# 20+ Guided Meditations For Deep Sleep, Anxiety & Self-Love (2 in 1):

Beginners Meditation & Positive Affirmations For Depression, Relaxation, Rapid Weight Loss, Overthinking & Energy

# 10 Hours Of Guided Meditations For Deep Sleep, Anxiety, Depression & Overthinking:

## Positive Affirmations & Meditation Scripts For Relaxation, Insomnia, Self-Love & Energy Healing

Healing Mindfulness & Hypnosis Buddy

© COPYRIGHT 2020 MY MAGIC MEDITATION- ALL RIGHTS RESERVED.

The content contained within this book may not be reproduced, duplicated or transmitted without direct written permission from the author or the publisher.
Under no circumstances will any blame or legal responsibility be held against the publisher, or author, for any damages, reparation, or monetary loss due to the information contained within this book. Either directly or indirectly.

Legal Notice:
This book is copyright protected. This book is only for personal use. You cannot amend, distribute, sell, use, quote or paraphrase any part, or the content within this book, without the consent of the author or publisher.

Disclaimer Notice:
Please note the information contained within this document is for educational and entertainment purposes only. All effort has been executed to present accurate, up to date, and reliable, complete information. No warranties of any kind are declared or implied. Readers acknowledge that the author is not engaging in the rendering of legal, financial, medical or professional advice. The content within this book has been derived from various sources. Please consult a licensed professional before attempting any techniques outlined in this book.
By reading this document, the reader agrees that under no circumstances is the author responsible for any losses, direct or indirect, which are incurred as a result of the use of the information contained within this document, including, but not limited to, — errors, omissions, or inaccuracies.

# Table Of Contents

Introduction ................................................................................................................. 5

Guided Mindfulness Meditation ................................................................................ 7

Guided Meditation for Deep Relaxation ................................................................. 12

Guided Meditation for Stress Relief ........................................................................ 17

Guided Meditation for Self-Healing ........................................................................ 23

Guided Meditation for Self-Healing While Sleeping .............................................. 29

# Introduction

In the modern world, we are often disconnected from our true selves and the divine power within us. Always busy, in a constant rush, trying to achieve everything and keep up with the world.
We forget about our true nature, about the ability of our magnificent bodies to heal themselves and maintain their perfect balance.
Too often, in our minds, we forget to notice the world around us and to really experience life - true life, here and now. Our minds constantly jump to the past and the future, skipping the present moment. We are so used to it that we don't even notice what's wrong with this picture.
Many of us can't stop our busy minds, and we have no idea that we choose our thoughts. Even worse, many of us are not even aware that we have thoughts that are not the truth.
We are not aware of what's going on within us, but we can see and feel the consequences—our bodies get sick, we feel bad about ourselves, and we suffer from issues on all levels.

**So how can meditation help?**
The popularity of meditation increases as more people discover the benefits of it. And there are many. You can use meditation to improve concentration and intellectual abilities, prevent memory loss, increase awareness, reduce stress or anxiety, improve sleep, change ways of thinking, build a positive mindset, and much more.

**Meditation can help you calm your mind.**
A calm and peaceful mind is where inner peace begins. However, most of us don't know how to turn off our constant stream of thoughts. Meditation helps you learn and practice that. That way, you become the master and your mind becomes a powerful servant that works for your highest good, as it's meant to be.

**It helps you de-stress.**
Stress is the number-one cause of most health and mental issues these days. There's no more efficient way to learn how to manage it, gain new perspectives on stressful situations, and protect yourself from chronic stress and its harmful effects on the body.

**It teaches you mindfulness.**
Have you ever wondered how much of life we miss out on while being focused on the past and future? A lot. Being mindful means being truly present and aware of everything—yourself and everything around you. Since the present moment is the only reality we have at any given moment, being consciously present improves your quality of life. Nothing can better teach you to be consciously aware of the present moment than mindfulness meditation.

**It helps you gain a deeper understanding and self-compassion.**
Meditation is also a way to reconnect with your inner self, your unconscious, and your higher self. Some forms of this practice can help you develop better self-understanding and support you in becoming a better version of yourself.

**Meditation helps you recharge, re-energize, and self-heal.**
Your body is wise; it's a part of a much bigger intelligence than yours. It knows how to heal itself and bring itself back into balance. You just need to calm your busy mind and move it into self-healing. Self-healing meditation is aimed at helping you learn how to do that, so you enhance your natural healing.

**Practicing meditation helps you change your way of thinking and develop a positive mindset.**

Thinking positive is a skill, and it can be learned and practiced. Meditation is a perfect way to see our thoughts for what they really are and to realize we have the power to choose which thoughts we want to follow.

**Meditation helps you improve your relationships.**

It increases patience, tolerance, kindness, understanding, and compassion, which are all key for building, maintaining, and improving connections with others.

There are so many benefits from practicing meditation that we could talk about it for days.

Here, you'll find guided meditations for developing mindfulness, deep relaxation, stress relief, and self-healing.

Remember that there's no wrong way to practice meditation. Just do your best to enjoy the moment.

# Guided Mindfulness Meditation

Welcome to guided mindfulness meditation.
Here and now—that's the only reality we really have. All other moments are just in our minds. Being truly present, here and now, means you're living the moment to its fullest. That means being mindful. Mindfulness means being consciously present in a moment and aware of everything going on within you and around you.
When you choose to consciously live as much as you can, you are choosing to improve your overall quality of life. Practicing mindfulness meditation will help you a great deal to reach that goal.
All you need to do is to follow my guidance that will help you ground yourself in the present moment. The main goal of this meditation is to wake your awareness of everything going on in your body and in your surroundings. That's why you need to calm your breathing, synchronize it with the rhythm of the universe, quiet your mind, and relax your body. Paying attention to the physical sensations within you will help you calm your mind and step out of your head.
Choose the time of the day when you can be alone and not disturbed. Find a quiet place and make yourself comfortable. It's important to feel the ease in your body so you can quiet your mind. Choose the position that suits you the most—you can either lie on a bed or on the floor, or you can sit on a floor, a chair, or a pillow. Just whatever you prefer and is convenient for you.
Make sure your clothes are comfortable, that all tight pieces of clothing, such as belts, are loosened, and that you are not too warm or too cold. If you want to practice this meditation before going to sleep, get ready for bed beforehand.
I suggest you practice this meditation with your eyes gently open. If you want to close them later during the meditation, that's okay—but try to stay alert.
To begin the meditation, choose one point in front of you and focus your vision on it. Narrow your focus on that point and allow everything else to fade away into the background.
Now, slowly broaden your field of view and allow the background to come into your sight.
Try to notice everything coming into your visual field without turning your head. Look consciously at everything in your sight. Try not to name the things you see, but just be aware of them and their characteristics. This might require some practice and time, but it's worth the effort. For instance, what colors do you see? Don't name them nor judge whether you like them or not. Just notice the colors, the shades, the textures, and the materials of the things in your sight. Notice as many tiny details as you can that you wouldn't have otherwise noticed.
The simplest things in life often turn out to be the best things. Breathing is one of them. It's incredibly simple—an essential life function—yet the most powerful way to ground you in the present.
Bring attention to your breathing. Notice its natural depth (or shallowness) and its rhythm. Just notice for now, without trying to control it. Listen to the sound of your breathing. Now, acknowledge any movements in your body connected to breathing.
Then, intentionally start to deepen your inhale and slow down your exhale.
Breathe in through your nose, counting to four. One, two, three, four.
Breathe out through the nose again, counting to six. One, two, three, four, five, six.
Repeat this breathing cycle a few times. Inhale—one, two, three, four.
Exhale—one, two, three, four, five, six.
Breathe in through your nose, counting to four—one, two, three, four.
Breathe out through the nose again, counting to six—one, two, three, four, five, six.

Breathing like this, with exhales longer than inhales, will relax you and tell your mind everything's okay. You can now rest and relax into the moment.

Take time to breathe consciously, being aware of everything about your breath, and maybe, for the first time, fully experience breathing.

Between every two breaths, there is a small pause. Focus on those still moments, the pauses between every two breaths. Feel the air filling your body and leaving it. Feel it goes into your nostrils and all the way into your lungs, then back outside.

Once again, breathe in—one, two, three, four. And breathe out—one, two, three, four, five, six.

If your regular breathing is shorter or longer than reflected in these numbers, don't worry. Don't force anything; just try to keep your exhales a bit longer than inhales.

There are certainly some thoughts going through your mind. That's perfectly normal and just how our minds work. Being consciously present means noticing them as well as your breathing. Be aware of the thoughts your mind is generating, yet don't engage with the thoughts. Just notice thoughts arise and let them pass by. Imagine your thoughts as colorful balloons flying away. As your breathing slows down, your mind slows down too. There are fewer and fewer balloons for you to release.

As mentioned earlier, pay special attention to pauses between each breath and, now, the similar pauses between your thoughts. Make a link between those two types of pauses in your mind. Allow yourself to be in this gap between every two breaths and every two thoughts. Allow your attention to rest in this space. If your thoughts are still wandering, and you notice that you tend to follow them, just bring your awareness back to your breath and the gap between breaths. Enjoy calm breathing and resting in the pauses.

Now, it is time to expand your awareness of your physical experience.

Invite your attention to your body. There's always so much you can experience on the physical level that you could stay in this moment, yet never grow bored.

Focus on your physical contact with the surface below you. You might experience this contact as warmth or pressure, or the physical border might feel blurred, giving you a feeling you're one with the surface beneath you. Feel your feet on the ground and your back being supported by the chair. If you are in a lying position, notice the surface under your whole body. Feel it supporting your back, your head, and the backs of your legs and arms.

Notice the surface's texture. Is it a flat floor, a soft mattress, a cushy chair, or a fuzzy cushion you're sitting on?

Acknowledge its temperature. Bring your attention to the surface of your body—your skin. Be aware of everything that touches your skin, from the brush of your clothes to the soft texture of your comforter, if you are lying down.

Feel the temperature of the space around you.

Be aware of any smells around you. Focus on each smell for a few moments. Again, try not to name them nor to judge them. Just notice them.

Bring your attention to the sounds around you. There are always many sounds surrounding us and our ears work all the time to process them. We are just used to ignoring most of them. So acknowledge everything you can hear. There might be sounds from outside—voices, traffic, birds, dog barks. Maybe there are sounds from appliances in your house. Or you might hear people in your apartment building. Listen to the sound of your breathing. Try to hear your heartbeat in your ears. Notice the details in the sounds you are can hear. There are always so many sounds around us, with numerous colors and tones; it's just a matter of whether we choose to ignore them or acknowledge them.

Take a deep breath. Breathe with your belly, so your belly expands on the inhale. Exhale as slowly as you can.

No need to do anything. Allow yourself to simply be. Just be present, in the moment, aware of everything within you and around you. You are a human being, not a human doing. You don't have to do something all the time. It's enough just to exist and be consciously aware right now. Feel the beat of your heart and the flow of your blood within you.

Bring awareness to the aliveness of all parts of your body. Nothing can ground one better than focusing on sensations in the body.

Take a deep breath, expanding your stomach like a balloon.

Breathe out, and focus on your hands. Feel the aliveness in your palms and fingers. Acknowledge all the sensations in these body part. You might feel warmth or tingling in them. If you feel the urge to move your hands or fingers, allow yourself to do it. Feel the movements and be aware of every sensation.

Move your focus to your arms. Notice all the sensations on the surface and within them, from your wrists to your shoulders. Feel the backside of your arms. Notice the temperature of the air around you. By focusing your awareness on a particular body part, you are already relaxing it.

Now bring your awareness to your feet and toes. Feel the tingling in your feet and toes, and how your awareness relaxes them. Allow this relaxed feeling to spread slowly upward to your ankles, your inner legs, knees, and upper legs. Acknowledge sensations in your whole legs—warmth, the brush of your clothes, the touch of the air. Allow your hips, glutes, and pelvic area to relax, and be consciously aware of all sensations in them.

Continue moving your awareness up to your stomach and chest. Be aware of the up-and-down movement of your stomach as it follows the rhythm of your breathing. Feel the air expanding your stomach and chest, and leaving it with your exhale. You might feel bubbles of air in your digestive system or hear sounds from your belly. Notice everything. Then pay undivided attention to the air going in and out of your body.

Breathe in to the count of four—one, two, three, four. Breathe out to the count of six—one, two, three, four, five, six.

Repeat this counting a few more times, focusing on the movement of air in through your nose, to the lungs, to your stomach, then all the way back.

Notice still periods between every two breaths. There's nothing there but pure existing. Feel grounded and allow yourself to relax further, sinking deeper into the surface.

When you notice thoughts running through your head, simpy acknowledge their existence. Imagine these thoughts are colorful balloons, so watch them and let them fly by. Resist the impulse to follow any of them. You might be used to following them, but you don't have to do that. Just stay out of it, observing them. You are not your thoughts. Your thoughts are not reality, nor they have any power over you. Acknowledge what they truly are—products of your mind.

Continue to scan all parts of your body. In doing so, you become aware of each part and your body as an integrated whole.

It's time to bring awareness to your back. Stretch your back and feel the texture of the furniture or floor beneath it. Pay attention to sensations in your back muscles. Scan them by focusing on each muscle, one by one, starting from your lower back. Straighten your spine, and notice the movement of the muscles following that straigthening. As you scan your muscles from the lowest point upwards, feel how they become heavier and softer. Feel the warmth and relief. If there is any tension remaining in your back, send love to that particular point and give it special attention. Visualize the tension melting, releasing all stress.

Now consciously feel your neck. Notice the weight of the head it carries all the time and the relief it feels while you're relaxing. Notice if the muscles of your neck are tensed, and bring focus to them.  Bring awareness to your throat. Notice the saliva in your throat and acknowledge the air going through your throat to reach your lungs.

Shift your attention to your head. First focus on the crown of your head. Have you ever be consciously aware of sensations in this part of your head? Relax your scalp, your ears, and your forehead. Be aware of any sensation, movement, and resistance. Feel the touch of hair brushing against your forehead and the temperature on your scalp. Take a deep breath in and visualize you are inhaling pure peace. Allow the air to spread throughout your head, relaxing it, then breathe out. Acknowledge any sensations that might arise within your head.

Focus on your face. Notice all sensations in your facial muscles. Too often, we keep our mouth, cheeks, and other facial muscles tensed all the time without even noticing. Scan your facial muscles with your full awareness. Become aware of any sensation in your eyes and the tiny muscles around your eyes. You can close your eyes if you want.

Take a few deep breaths, visualizing that you are inhaling peace and tranquility. With your exhale, let go of everything that isn't serving your peace of mind and body. Let your exhale take away all the tension in your body and feel your body relaxing as it does. Let your body sink into the surface beneath you, completely supported by it.

Notice the temperature of the air around you. Feel it with your lips, forehead, palms, and lower legs.

Once again, ask yourself what can you hear around you and within you. Try to count all the sounds you can hear. Don't name them or think about them. Just focus on the sounds coming into your ears.

If there is any area of your body that is not relaxed yet, give it special attention. It is trying to tell you something. Sometimes, giving special attention to a tight or unpleasant sensation in our body is enough to make it soften and fade away. Notice the sensation and stay with it for some time, although it might feel unpleasant. If your mind wanders and tries to get busy thinking, gently bring your attention back to the present moment and stay with the experience of the sensation.

Take a deep breath. Exhale slowly. Concentrate only on your breath.

Inhale again. Exhale.

Take a breath again. Slowly exhale through your mouth.

Feel the fresh cool air entering your nostrils and traveling throughout your body. Exhale. Feel the warmth of the air, leaving your body.

Imagine what's going on within your body now – your organs, your muscles, your bones, your nervous system – and watch them all relax. You're giving them time to heal and recharge. Notice your heartbeat and your breathing. Acknowledge the relaxing feeling within the whole body.

Inhale peace. Exhale tension.

Inhale consciousness. Exhale ignorance.

Inhale calmness. Exhale stress.

Inhale clarity. Exhale chaos.

Inhale tranquility. Exhale worries.

Inhale ease. Exhale effort.

Inhale energy. Exhale tiredness.

You are consciously present and aware of this moment, as it is right now. Now you know what it is to be mindful. This moment is the only reality that exists for you. The past and the future are just stories, existing only in your mind. You can feel and experience so much at this very moment. This moment is real, and your thoughts are not. Thoughts are just random creations of your mind. If you still have any thoughts left in your mind, imagine the thought as a balloon you're holding. Open your hand and let it fly away. If you still have stubborn thoughts that refuse to leave you, imagine them as a bunch of balloons you are holding. Now let them all fly into the sky. Whenever you notice that you're following your thoughts and are about to lose conscious presence, bring your attention back to your breathing, surroundings, and the sensations in your body.

When you are completely aware and grounded in the present, you are fully alive. You have your body, mind, and spirit together in one place, and so you become incredibly powerful.

Take another full breath again. Fill your stomach and your chest with peace and calmness. Breathe out as slowly as you can, aware of each moment as you do so.

Now, when you feel ready, you can return to your usual activities. You'll notice that you become more and more mindful and consciously aware of everything you do and everything that goes on in each day of your life.

# Guided Meditation for Deep Relaxation

Welcome to the meditation that will help you relax both your body and mind, and achieve a deeper level of serenity and awareness. It's one of the best things you can do for yourself whenever you feel stressed, tensed, or just want to enjoy some deep peace and calmness.

Relaxation is a precious gift we can give ourselves, and its positive effects are tremendous. Most of us go through life tensed, lacking moments of relaxation in our everyday life, not even being aware of the weight we carry around.

We hold stress and tension in our bodies, poisoning ourselves from the inside out. All that accumulated negativity creates energy blocks, which prevents us from fulfilling our true potential and living magnificent lives.

Our bodies and minds need relaxation on a regular basis. So much good is happening when we regularly practice relaxation. By doing so, we open up to the flow of energy and invite prosperity to come into our lives. Practicing relaxing meditation, you'll experience benefits in all fields of life.

Allowing yourself to relax completely is the best thing you can do for yourself and the people around you.

This is time only for you. You deserve it. Relaxation will improve your success in everything you do and the quality of your life in general. So allow yourself to enjoy these moments and being part of the process.

I invite you to follow my guidance.

All you need is some quiet space where you can be alone and not disturbed for a chunk of time. Choose whatever time of day or evening you like. Make sure the temperature of the space around you is pleasant, and use a warm blanket if need be.

Use a few moments in the beginning to find a comfortable position and settle into it. You can either sit or lie down. Take a few breaths, and try to ground yourself in the present moment.

Close your eyes and give yourself permission to take this relaxing journey.

Just listen to my voice, which will gently lull you to a state of deep relaxation. Once you feel completely relaxed, you can easily drift off to sleep, or just enjoy this state, and then slowly get back to your usual activities.

Take a few deep breaths to ground yourself. Breathe in through your nose, into the belly. Hold it for a moment, and then slowly breathe out through your mouth.

Try to exhale as slowly as you can. When your exhales are longer than your inhales, you are sending signals to your brain that you are safe and all is well. Your mind receives the message and, in turn, sends out signals to relax your body. This technique can help you in everyday life whenever you feel the need to calm down and feel grounded. Simple, yet super-efficient. Breathe in through your nose to your belly, then breathe out as slowly as you can. Repeat.

Breathe in. Slowly breathe out through your mouth. Do it again. Feel grounded, feel present, here and now. Allow yourself to relax and enjoy these moments. This is time only for you, this experience is pure joy, and you deserve it.

Now, once your breathing is slower, deeper, and calm, allow it to flow in its natural pattern.

Observe your breathing. Notice the movement of your breath. Feel the air entering your nostrils and traveling through your body, down, into your lungs. Feel it expanding your abdomen, then releasing, going all the way back out through your mouth. Your breath is always with you. You can focus on it at any time and bring yourself into peace.

If you have an expectation about wanting something special to happen during meditation, release that expectation. Don't expect anything to happen, any change to come, or any insights to pop up. Focus only on the present moment and be completely aware of it. This is time reserved for relaxation, along with a complete recharge and restoration of your energy. You don't have to think now. You don't need to be productive or to do anything other than relax now. Give your mind permission to stop and relax now.

If this seems impossible, don't stress yourself about it. Most of us have no idea how to stop our minds and are used to our minds being busy all the time. And that's okay—your mind needs some time to develop this relaxation skill. So don't be concerned if you still have some thoughts going through your brain or some internal chatter. It's not unusual to have inner chatter and other thoughts. What you need to focus on is observing these thoughts and inner chatter instead of engaging with them. Notice, but don't engage. Just let them go. With practice, this will become easier. Notice the thought, and let it go. Random thoughts will still pop up, but they'll fade away into the background once you don't engage. Don't worry; your mind is used to producing numerous thoughts, and, if you are consistent with meditation practice, it will learn with time to relax and rest from thinking.

Now imagine you're walking in the sunshine. It's a beautiful day. Feel the warmth on your skin. The sky is blue and the air is fresh. You're walking up a green hill. The temperature is just right, and you feel as if the air is gently wrapping around your skin. You easily get to the top of the hill. The sight is magical. You can gaze at distant mountains and a dark blue river down in a valley.

Imagine you are lying down on the ground. The sky above you is clear, with just a few feathery clouds in sight. The grass below you is thick and soft, like a comfy mattress. You feel as if you could fall asleep like a baby in the cradle, listening to the birds' singing. Being supported by this grassy pillow, you feel absolutely safe and peaceful.

You can smell the freshness of the air from the hills. It's so pure that you can almost see it shimmering. Take a deep breath, filling your body with sparkling air. Exhale slowly, feeling your whole body relaxing on the soft pillow of grass.

Now, it's time for your body to relax completely, part by part. Bring your attention to your toes. Breathe in, and, as you breathe out, relax your toes, one by one. Relax your feet and let them slightly open up towards the sky. Relax your ankles. Bring your awareness slowly upward to your legs. Feel the grass below your legs. Relax your knees, and then move up to your thigh muscles. Relax those heavy thigh muscles. Feel the texture of the ground on the backs of your legs and glutes. Feel how your muscles become heavier with each breath. Allow your hips to relax and the muscles of your glutes to loosen.

Now, bring awareness to your hands. Our hands do so much for us. They serve us every single day of our lives. They truly deserve rest and relaxation.

Now, place your hands beside your body , with your palms opened to the sky. First, let's relax your fingers, one by one. Breathe in, and, breathing out, relax your fingers. Relax each of your fingers, one by one. Feel the sensations in your fingers; be aware of the tension leaving them. Now, relax your palms and your wrists.

Too often in life, we strongly hold onto things. Usually things that don't serve us. These things might be our thoughts, beliefs, habits, directions, or opinions. These things all come from our ego, and if you truly want to set yourself free, it's time to let them go. Open your hands, relax them, and let off everything you've been holding onto—not just literally, but figuratively, too.

When you let go of everything you've been holding onto, you set yourself free from old, stagnant energy and open up space for wonderful new things to flow into your life. By relaxing and opening your hands, you're welcoming all of that.

Now, relax your forearms, and feel the grass and the ground below them. Bring awareness to your elbows and notice them becoming soft. Release all the tension from the muscles of your arms, and feel them becoming flexible and relaxed.

Now, put the focus on your abdomen, and relax it. Bring your attention to your belly, and notice how it expands with every breath in and empties with each breath out. Your stomach is so relaxed that you can imagine it as a balloon, easily expanding and shrinking in the rhythm of your breathing. There's no effort and no need to control your breathing. Just watch your totally relaxed belly, moving up and down, up and down.

Now, bring awareness to your chest. With each exhale, relax your chest a bit more. Feel your ribcage floating, light yet heavy at the same time.

Now, bring awareness to your back muscles. Relax those muscles, from your lower back to the back of your shoulders.

Starting from your glutes and moving upward, relax all your back muscles, one by one. Imagine your vertebrae in perfect alignment. Visualize your breath going through your spine. Inhale through your spine, and, while exhaling, relax the muscle you're focusing on. With each exhale, your back loosens and relaxes more and more. Feel the press of the ground's surface beneath your back. Notice its structure and temperature. Feel your back muscles become heavy, giving up on any effort, letting the surface support them completely.

The single most important part of this relaxation is relaxing your shoulders. It's time to relax them now. Release your shoulders from your ears, letting them get back into a relaxed position.

The shoulders are where we hold most of our tension, stress, and worries. They carry most of the weight. We are not even aware of this. Letting your shoulders relax is showing yourself that it's truly safe to rest and relax. You are not supposed to be worried and stressed all the time. You deserve to rest. Your shoulders will thank you for this. Let all the weight fall off them and fade away. Enjoy the sense of being free from any weight, worries, anger, and rage. Enjoy being light and free. Your shoulders are recovering and re-energizing now, free from any duty. They don't have to be tensed anymore to carry all the negativity. They don't even need to hold and carry your head—all of that is left to the surface below you now.

You can relax your neck now—both the back of your neck and your throat. Allow your throat to open up and soften.

Your head is resting on the fresh grass, and the grass feels like a fluffy, comfortable pillow. Relax the back of your head. Let your scalp relax, and then your forehead.

Relax your ears. Hear everything that is around you—the soft wind in the grass, birds, and insects around you, the rhythm of your own breathing, and your heart pumping blood throughout your body. Your ears are always on duty, even while you sleep. Allow them to relax now.

Relax your face, including all the tiny muscles that are tensed all the time. Let your cheeks relax. No one is watching, so don't worry about how you look. Let your jaw release, and let your mouth slightly open. Bring awareness to your mouth. Relax your lips, and then your mouth on the inside. Allow your tongue to relax, from its top to its base. Notice how relaxed your cheeks, mouth, your tongue, and your throat are.

Focus on the top of your nose, and visualize how it relaxes, along with your cheeks.

Now, release all the tension from your eyebrows. Relax the forehead, and allow the muscles of your forehand to fall. Focus on the tiny muscles around your eyes, and relax them.

Now, calm your eyes. It might require some time and practice, but do it as best you can. Don't worry if you still can't completely calm and soften your eyes. Allow your eyes to sink into your head. It's incredibly relaxing to calm and rest your eyes. It feels so good.

Focus on the top of your head. Allow your skull to relax.

Now, bring your awareness to the biggest organ in your body - your skin. Your skin is there to cover and protect you, to feel touch and temperature for you, to protect you from the outside world and connect you with it at the same time. Give your skin the rest, relaxation, and restoration it deserves. So, visualize relaxing your skin, from the skin on your toes to the top of your head. Feel the texture of the surface beneath your body. Allow your skin on the back of your body to relax, too.

Imagine your body relaxing on the inside as well. Visualize your internal organs relaxing and resting. Imagine each organ, then each tiny cell of your body, relaxing and rejuvenating. Every system in your body is releasing all its tension and toxins, repairing itself, and filling with fresh, vital energy.

Now, your whole body is relaxed. Enjoy that feeling of complete relaxation and deep rest.

Focus on your breathing again. Notice its rhythm without trying to control it. It feels so good to be there, completely present and aware, deeply relaxed, and just breathing. Smile to yourself and appreciate this precious moment.

Your body is thanking you now. Mentally say thanks to this moment of deep serenity, to your breath for keeping you alive, to the ground for supporting your body. Feel connected with the surface of the ground and strongly anchored into it.

It's time to let go of everything that's not serving your highest good. Visualize all the weight you've been carrying along with all dark emotions leaving your body and being absorbed by the ground below you. All dark thoughts, all worries, and all doubts—you can name them. Tell them: *I'm letting you go now*, and do it. The ground will receive them. You can repeat this process as many times as you want, with every dark thought, every concern, everything you don't want in your mind and body anymore.

You might notice that your mind is not as calm and relaxed as your body. Don't worry—it's normal to have some thoughts, as it's the mind's job to produce them. Just observe the thoughts, and notice them come and go, come and go. Allow your mind to relax. It doesn't have to grab and follow each thought. This requires some practice, and you'll become better at just observing, not engaging. This is your time for relaxation, not for solving problems, analyzing, or any thinking. Keep your mind out of your thoughts. Just observe them, and let go. By allowing your mind to rest without engaging in your thoughts, you see your thoughts for what they really are. None of them is fact—they are just products of your mind. None of them has any power besides the power you give them.

Now, visualize the blue sky above you. It's a beautiful sunny day. The day is nice, but you notice clouds here and there. Most of them are white and fluffy, but there are also some grayish ones. You already know that those clouds represent your thoughts. Some clouds are light and positive, while others are dark and heavy. As different thoughts pop up in your mind, you see more clouds in the sky. Just watch them float away.

You can feel the freshness of the air and the breeze on your skin. The breeze must be much stronger high in the sky, as you can see clouds are moving much faster now. They all go with the wind and then disappear from your sight.

They fly away, one by one, leaving the sky clear and light blue. You feel peace. Your inner space is exactly like the sky above you. Your mind is calm without the urge to create or follow thoughts. You're enjoying deep inner peace.

It's time to get up. You are standing on the top of the hill, looking at the valley and distant mountains. The fresh breeze has turned into wind. It's pretty cold now, but you enjoy it. You're filling your lungs and belly with fresh mountain air. This wind is not ordinary. It has cleansing power, and it will take away everything you want it to. So it's time to let go everything you don't want anymore.

Take a deep breath, and then with the exhale, let go of any tension that remains. Breathe out any negative thoughts, stress, worries, or fears. Let it all go with the wind—any old, outgrown beliefs, limiting thoughts, or stagnant energy. Let go of all that. Release all hard feelings and bitterness. Let them all go into nothingness.

You can feel the cool wind becoming stronger, and now it blows through your clothes and your body. It blows through your skin, your muscles, and bones, carrying away everything you don't want to hold anymore. You stand in this cleansing wind. Enjoy this unique experience. With each exhale, get rid of all the weight and negativity inside you. Let the pure wind carry away everything that's holding you back. Fill your lungs, your stomach, and both your mental and physical inner space with purity and fresh energy, new thoughts, fresh ideas, and positivity.

With every breath in, name one thing you want to get more of: health, peace, well-being, love, happiness, and so on.

With every breath out, name one thing you want to release: stress, fear, anger, and so on.

Breathe in, and say to yourself what you're filling your inner space with. For instance, you can breathe in, then say "health."

Breathe out, and release all the physical and mental issues you want to get rid of.

Inhale peace, exhale tension.

Inhale wealth. Exhale worries.

Repeat this as many times as you wish, for everything you want to be carried away and everything you want to have more of in your life.

Be one with the cleansing wind; be the active part of this process. When you let go of everything you want, the cleansing is done. You are free from any weight and negativity, and filled with new, vibrant energy.

The wind calms, turning once again into a soft breeze. You feel fresh and energized. Your mind is clean and calm. Your body is entirely relaxed and re-energized. You feel like you are reborn.

You can enjoy this feeling for as long as you want. From this point of complete relaxation, you can drift off to sleep if it's night, or open your eyes, gently move and stretch your body, then get up slowly and move on with your usual activities.

You can come back to this green hill with fresh grass and a cool breeze whenever you want to relax, take a pause from the outside world, and gain new energy.

# Guided Meditation for Stress Relief

Welcome to the meditation for stress relief. We are so used to living with constant stress that we don't even notice how it affects our lives. Although a certain amount of stress doesn't do any harm, living with chronic stress is exhausting. It drains our vital energy and causes harm to all our life fields, especially our health.

That's why we need to rest and recover from it regularly. There are many wonderful ways to ease stress and reduce its amount in our lives, such as getting a massage and enjoying a hobby. Meditation is among the most efficient techniques for relieving stress.

Relieve your stress intentionally whenever you feel the need. Doing so will reap miracles for your quality of life.

My voice will be your companion on this journey and will help you calm, relax, and lower your level of stress. You can practice this meditation whenever you feel stressed. Also, feel free to choose particular techniques as applied here to calm yourself before or after stressful events.

Our nature is to be relaxed and in peace. Our bodies and minds have the power to recharge and repair themselves. But as we are stressed all the time, we don't allow them to do so. That's why everyone needs some time to decompress and relax. Don't consider this "me-time" selfish or a waste of time. On the contrary, consider it an investment in your quality of life.

We are taught it's only okay to be busy, productive, and stressed all the time. Give yourself permission to return to your true nature. Allow yourself to spend enough time in peace to process experiences, recharge, and heal yourself.

To begin, find a quiet place and time of day when you can remove yourself from any distractions. Find a comfortable position and follow my guidance.

Stress affects all levels of our being. The most obvious levels are our body, our mind, and our breathing. To relieve stress, we'll focus on those three levels. This meditation will help you calm your mind, relax your body, and deepen your breathing, restoring your lost balance.

Focusing on your breathing first will help you turn your attention inward. Then, we'll relax your body, and, in the end, you'll relax your mind.

When you begin the meditation, you might notice there are many thoughts randomly popping up in your head. Don't stress yourself about them, and don't try to stop them. Just let them pass by.

Just be present, fully aware of this moment and place. Don't expect anything special to happen. Just be open to whatever this experience brings you.

Know that it's okay to have thoughts. It's expected to have thoughts during meditation, and don't stress about it.

Allow yourself to simply be here. Let go of any expectations and inner judgment. Focus on this very moment and be open to whatever it brings you.

Find a comfortable position. You can lie down or sit, but just make sure your back is straight. If you are lying down, your spine should be straight yet relaxed. If you are sitting, also make sure your spine is straight yet relaxed. Once you feel comfortable, close your eyes and take a few deep breaths.

Bring awareness to your breathing.

Pay your undivided attention to your breath—from the moment it enters your nostrils, as it moves all throughout your body, and all the way out. Feel the air in your nose and notice its flow down to your lungs. Feel the air filling your stomach, expanding your abdomen. Then, notice the air leaving your belly and follow it all the way back. Feel the warm air leaving your body through the nose. Be aware of any movement in your body connected with your breathing. Our breathing is magnificent—so simple, yet precious. It keeps us alive even though we hardly ever pay attention to it. Even when it seems like nothing special is happening, there's so much going on in our bodies. Your breath is always with you until the end of your life. You can bring your attention back to it anytime, grounding yourself in the present moment and getting your power back.

Now, try to notice all the sensations breathing provokes in your body. It's time to deepen your breath by counting.

Breathe in, counting to four—one, two, three, four.

Then hold the breath to the count of three—one, two, three.

Breathe out, to the count of six—one, two, three, four, five, six.

Breathe in, counting to four—one, two, three, four.

Then hold the breath to the count of three—one, two, three.

Breathe out, to the count of six—one, two, three, four, five, six.

Let's repeat that once again.

Inhale, counting to four—one, two, three, four.

Hold your breath—one, two, three.

Exhale to the count of six—one, two, three, four, five, six.

Breathe in again, and while you're doing so, visualize that you are gathering all the stress from your body. Collect all the stress and tension you can, from all your body parts.

Now, visualize you are blowing out a dandelion and breathe out as slowly as you can. With the exhale, let go of all the stress you collected.

Breathing in, visualize you are inhaling calmness and peace. Fill your nose, your lungs, and your stomach with tranquility. Breathe out slowly, mentally saying to yourself: *calm.*

Taking another deep breath, breathe in calmness and peace. Breathe out slowly, saying to yourself: *relax.*

Repeat this series a few times. Enjoy this tranquil, deep, and slow breathing and releasing all the stress. If any thought comes into your mind (and it certainly will), just notice it and let it go. Bring your focus back to your breath, following its way through the body and the physical sensations it causes.

Mindful and conscious breathing is a practice that greatly reduces stress and helps relaxation. Since your breath is always with you, you can use it whenever you want to.

Stress affects us on so many levels—not only our breathing, but also our minds and bodies. It causes issues with blood pressure, heart, organ function, and even skin appearance. Although our bodies have the ability to heal themselves, they are unable to do so when we are stressed. That's why it's crucial to learn how to decompress and release the stress from your body, and to practice it regularly.

When you manage to calm and relax your body, you are sending signals to your mind that it's safe for it to relax as well.

Now, it's time to relax the body by tensing and loosening it part by part.

To start, bring your awareness to your toes. Breathe in and tense up your feet. Hold the breath while the muscles are still tensed, counting: *three, two, one*. Then exhale and release, relaxing your toes and feet.

Taking the next breath, pay attention to your legs. Tense your lower legs and knees. Still holding them tensed, hold your breath and count: *three, two, one*. And release, letting the muscles relax.

Take another deep breath, tensing your upper legs and hips. Hold the breath, keeping them tensed as tightly as you can, and count: *three, two, one*. And, exhaling, relax the muscles completely.

With the next inhale, tighten your glutes. While holding them tensed, count: *three, two, one*. Then exhale, relaxing the glute muscles.

Breathe in and clench your fists. Hold them clenched to the count of three—*three, two, one*. Breathing out, relax your fingers and hands. Relax your wrists and let your hands open up to the ceiling.

With the next inhale, tighten your arms. Feel the tension in your elbows and upper arms. Hold them tensed to the count of three—*three, two one*. Relax your arms.

Inhale, and tense up your shoulders, lifting them up so that they almost touch your ears. Keeping them lifted, count backward: *three, two, one*. Then slowly exhale, relaxing your shoulders. Allow them to drop down and release all the tension and weight they've been carrying.

Take another breath and tighten your stomach. Contract your abdominal muscles so tightly to pull your navel to your spine. Hold the muscles tensed as tightly as you can while holding your breath. Count: *three, two, one*, and relax. Allow your breathing to return to its natural pattern and your belly to its natural, relaxed position.

With the next breath, fill up your lungs and tense up the muscles of your chest. Hold your breath, counting *three, two, one*. Breathe out and allow your chest to relax. Feel your chest completely relax, as though your ribcage were floating.

Breathe in and tighten the muscles of your lower back. Straighten up your spine, and feel the tension. Hold your breath to the count of three: *three, two, one*. Then breathe out, releasing tension and relaxing the muscles of your lower back.

With the next inhale, tense the muscles in the middle part of your back. Hold them tensed to the count of three: *three, two, one*. Then breathe out, and relax them fully.

Now, feel the tension in your upper back. The upper back is where we hold a lot of pressure and stress. Now, tense the muscles of the upper back and feel all your muscles tighten. Hold your breath, counting: *three, two, one*. Breathe out, and relax all the muscles of the upper back.

Move on to the back of your neck and feel it tensed as you breathe in. Hold your breath—*three, two, one*. Breathe out and relax the muscles of your neck. Feel the relief releasing tension.

Breathe in, visualizing your scalp tightening. Feel the tension in your scalp. Although it's unpleasant, stay with this sensation to the count of three while holding your breath—*three, two, one*. Then breathe out slowly and relax your scalp.

Tense up your forehead. This area is often much too tensed, due to worry or overthinking. You can try to tense it even more by raising your eyebrows. Hold the forehead as tensed as you can, and count: *three, two, one*. Breathe out, and let your forehead relax.

Take a deep breath, and try to tense your eye muscles and squeeze the eyes. Hold them like that—*Three, two, one.* Breathe out, loosening the muscles around your eyes, and allow your eyes to soften and sink into the head. Allow all tension to drift away. It feels so good to calm your eyes.

With the next breath in, clench your jaw. Hold it for a moment: *three, two, one*. Breathe out, and let your jaw drop. Allow your mouth to open up slightly so your teeth aren't touching. Relax your lips. Allow your tongue to drop back, relaxed, and relax the very base of it.

Your whole body is relaxed now. Breathe deeply and mentally scan your body once again. Notice if there's tension anywhere. If you feel some part of your body is still tensed, bring awareness to that part and intentionally relax it as you did above by tensing and relaxing it.

If you notice any tension remaining in any part of your body, visualize that you're setting it free, allowing it to get to the surface. Imagine all the remaining stress collecting on your skin. From here, the stress will float away with your breathing.

Since your mind is relaxed now, your body is getting signals that everything's fine, you are safe, and it's safe for your body to relax fully.

Your breathing is calm, deep, and slow. Your body is deeply relaxed. Now, it's time to relax your mind as well.

The mind is exactly where most of our stress comes from. Our minds are used to being busy all the time. Since they produce tons of thoughts at every moment, our minds are stressed, overwhelmed, and occupied with worries, tasks, scenarios, fears, and all sorts of trash. We are in a constant rush, so we don't leave enough time for our minds to decompress, slow down, and recharge. That is the main cause of many, many problems. For instance, most of our health-related come from the inability of our minds to rest and heal. That's why it's crucial to learn how to soothe and relax your mind. Every part of our body needs some time to rest and repair, even dedicated workers like our brains.

If you notice that your mind is full of all sorts of thoughts running in all directions, don't be upset by that. Your mind is used to doing that, and you can't just turn it off as if you're pressing a button.

Instead, take a deep breath.

When the next thought arises in your mind, just notice it. Resist the urge to follow it. You don't have to engage in each thought that pops up in your head. Just notice it and, with your exhale, let it go. Repeat the same with the next thought. And the next thought.

As you do this, you'll notice your thoughts slow down. The rhythm of your breathing becomes the one that sets the pace.

It can also help if you imagine your thoughts as balloons. When your thoughts are balloons, they float to you. You catch them gently for a moment and then let go, watching them float away. Some of them will float to you quickly, some of them float to you more slowly. Eventually, you'll do the same with all of them, letting them go and watching them fly away.

As you go on with this practice—breathing, noticing, and letting go—you'll notice that your thoughts became slower and lighter. They will look lighter, like soap bubbles or feathers. Notice the feather floating to you. Just blow it away and watch it pass by.

For every dark, hard thought that bothers you and causes you stress, visualize a small, dark cloud in the sky. Depending on how stressful or hard a thought is, give it a proper dark shade, from light gray to black. Repeat this for all of the thoughts that stress you out. Once you've mentally placed all of them in the sky, it's time to let them go. Watch your imagined dark clouds. Take a deep breath, and, breathing out, release the dark clouds.

Once you are done with sending your stress to the sky, it's time for relief. Watch your stressful thought and the dark cloud you created for it. Breathe in, and, as you breathe out, imagine you are releasing all the stress. While doing so, watch how all the darkness is leaving the cloud. Its color turns lighter and lighter until it is entirely white and fluffy.

Repeat this with the next thought and cloud. Breathe in, gathering all the stress and darkness. Breathe out, let go, and watch the cloud become snow-white.

With the next in-breath, take up all the darkness from the next cloud and release it all with your out-breath.

Repeat this practice for a while. Repeat it with every stressful thought and dark cloud until all of the clouds become snow-white, light, and feathery. There's nothing hard or dark in your mind anymore.

Feel how light and at ease you are. Feel free from any stressful thoughts, and enjoy this feeling.

Once more, take a deep breath, and, as you exhale, visualize yourself blowing the first white cloud away. It flows away pretty fast, as if there's a strong wind in the sky, and disappears in the distance. In the place where it used to be, there's clear blue sky now. Again, breathe in deeply, and, as you breathe out, blow the next cloud away.

Do this for as long as you need to clear all the clouds from the sky.

Now, the sky above you is clear and light blue—the same as your mind. It's calm, light, and clear. You feel ease and serenity. Your mind is deeply relaxed now.

Now, with your body deeply relaxed and your mind completely calm, pull your attention back to your breathing. You don't need to control your breathing, or count it. Just observe your natural, calm, and deep breathing. Breathe in through your nose and breathe out through your mouth, mentally saying these affirmations to yourself as you do so:

Take a deep breath. *I am relaxed.* Breathe out.
Breathe in. *I am calm.* Breathe out.
Breathe in. *I am at ease.* Breathe out.
Breathe in. *I am tranquil.* Breathe out.
Breathe in. *I am wonderful.* Breathe out.
Breathe in. *I am at peace with everything outside and within me.* Breathe out.
Breathe in. *I feel all the cells of my body are relaxed now.* Breathe out.
Breathe in. *I am confident.* Breathe out.
Breathe in. *I am skilled.* Breathe out.
Breathe in. *I am focused.* Breathe out.
Breathe in. *I can handle anything that life brings me.* Breathe out.
Breathe in. *There is peace within me.* Breathe out.
Breathe in. *I am relaxed.* Breathe out.
Breathe in. *I am intelligent.* Breathe out.
Breathe in. *I am calm.* Breathe out.
Breathe in. *I bring light and ease with me wherever I go.* Breathe out.
Breathe in *I am powerful.* Breathe out.
Breathe in. *I can handle everything with ease.* Breathe out.
Breathe in. *I am in harmony.* Breathe out.

Continue repeating the following affirmations as you breathe in and out.
*I am calm.*
*I am relaxed.*
*I am at ease.*
*I am tranquil.*
*I am confident.*
*I am skilled.*
*I am focused.*
*I can handle anything that life brings me.*
*There is peace within me.*
*I am intelligent.*
*I am calm.*
*I am wonderful.*
*I am at peace with everything outside and within me.*
*I feel all the cells of my body are relaxed now.*
*I bring light and ease with me wherever I go.*
*I am powerful.*
*I can handle everything with ease.*
*I am in harmony.*
*I am at peace, completely relaxed now.*
Your body is now relaxed from the top of your head to your toes.

Bring awareness to the contact of your body with the surface beneath you. Visualize the surface as an incredibly comfortable cloud. It's exactly the same size as your body, and it's here to support you and cradle your relaxed body. This cloud is the comfiest place you've ever reclined on. Enjoy resting on it.

The cloud slowly moves higher, taking you off the ground. You are relaxed, knowing you're safe. So you're resting completely on the cloud that takes you up to the sky.

You're looking at the ground. From here, everything looks tiny, as if it's all made from Legos. You can see colorful land, cities, woods, fields, mountains, rivers, and oceans.

Now, try to locate all those things that used to stress you out. You can't even find them, so tiny they are. Can you even imagine how insignificant they are? All those worries and concerns that used to bother you, they're smaller than a speck of dust. You can't even see them from your safe, fluffy cloud. Here, you feel no stress or worries on your personal relaxing cloud—only calmness, serenity, and deep relaxation.

Suddenly, you notice your cloud begins to shine with golden light. The light becomes brighter, and you realize it's shining from the center of the cloud. It looks as if the sun is shining through the cloud, as if it's at the center of the cloud. With each moment, the light becomes stronger, and the whole cloud shines brightly now. You can feel the pleasant warmth as the light enters your body and spreads through it. You look at your feet and notice they glow, and now your legs are shining with this golden light. The light is moving upwards through your body, reaching your stomach and chest. Your hands and arms are now glowing. Now your head is radiating the light. Your whole body shines. You can also feel the light spreading inside you on the inside, bathing your internal organs, filling your heart and your blood.

The light has cleansing, relaxing, and healing powers. It's the remedy for any type of stress. You are full of shimmering golden light, and you radiate it all around you, spreading peace and calmness. This deep peace is far bigger than yourself; it's everywhere, within and around you. It wraps and covers you like a cozy blanket, comforting and further relaxing your mind and body, thoughts, emotions, and every cell in your body.

If there's still any dark and stress remaining anywhere within you, it's been dissolved now by the divine golden light.

Enjoy the experience of bathing in the healing golden light. Stress is just a distant memory now. You don't have to experience it ever again. Instead, you can come back to this deep peace whenever you want. Whenever you feel stressed, you can rest and relax on your cloud and bathe in golden light.

You are absolutely relaxed now. All the stress has left you. Your body is completely relaxed, your mind is calm and clear, and your breathing is deep and slow. You are at ease.

Your cloud gently lands on the ground.

You slowly move your hands, then your legs. You gently stretch your body and open your eyes. When you are ready, you get up from your cloud.

You are relaxed and re-energized now, free from stress. From here, you can drift off to sleep or get back to your daily activities.

# Guided Meditation for Self-Healing

Welcome to the guided meditation for self-healing. Every one of us has the ability to heal ourselves. Sometimes we just need to be reminded of this power. This meditation is aimed at helping you awaken your abilities to heal yourself.

Whether you have a severe diagnosis or other health issue, or you just don't feel very well, this meditation will help you. You'll gain benefits from it immediately after finishing it. Regular practice of this meditation can ease even serious conditions and make severe illness disappear.

You might not be completely aware of this power within you—a power that can help you heal the worst conditions. That power is the same as the divine power that created you.

Our natural state is balance. Our bodies have the ability to repair themselves and to keep themselves in harmony. Problems with health are often consequences of being out of balance for a while and not being aligned with the divine power within us. The good news is that this process works in the opposite direction as well. So if you succeed in restoring the lost balance back, your health will immediately improve.

But your body and mind need some peace and quiet time to heal and repair. If you are always busy and active—in a constant rush, often stressed, never completely relaxed—your body has no time to recharge and repair itself. That's why meditation is the perfect way to enhance your self-healing power. Your body is naturally wise, and it knows how to work magnificent things without your engagement. All you need to do to help it is to move it out of the way and allow your body to open to what's the best for it. Your busy mind is the main obstacle in this natural process of self-healing. It needs to be calmed so your body can regenerate.

The main goal of this meditation is to remind your body how to heal itself, and to calm your mind. Throughout this meditation, you will learn how to relax your whole body, calm your mind, slow and deepen your breathing, show appreciation and love to your body, and remind your body of its natural self-healing powers.

You can practice this meditation at any time. For the best results, however, I recommend you do it regularly. It is most efficient to practice it as a part of your evening or morning routine.

Whatever time you choose, make sure you won't be disturbed for about an hour. Dedicate this time to yourself and your healing, and make this time a priority. Pause all distractions, and turn off notifications and ringers.

Lie down and find the comfiest position for yourself. If it's more convenient, you can also sit. However, I recommend you do this meditation lying down and using earphones for the best experience.

To empower your body to use its self-healing abilities, you must achieve a state of deep relaxation first. To reach that state, pay attention to my voice and follow my guidance.

First, make sure you're comfortable and pleasantly warm. Straighten your back and straighten your legs, spreading your legs slightly apart from each other. Straighten your hands beside the body. Before we begin, ground yourself with a few deep breaths.

Intentionally slow your breathing. Make sure your exhales are longer than your inhales. That way, you're sending signals to your mind that everything is OK and it's safe for you to relax.

Take a breath through your nose to the count of four—one, two, three, four. Breathe out through your mouth to the count of eight—one, two, three, four, five, six, seven, eight.

Repeat it. Breathe in, counting one, two, three, four. Breathe out, counting one, two, three, four, five, six, seven, eight.

Do it once again. Inhale—one, two, three, four.
Exhale—one, two, three, four, five, six, seven, eight.
If your breathing can't reach these numbers, don't worry. Do your best, especially focusing on the long exhales.
The main thing now is being gentle with yourself. So don't force yourself in any way; there's no such thing as being unsuccessful in meditation.
Allow your breathing to return to its natural pattern.
With every inhale, visualize the air you breathe is white, healing light. With each exhale, let go of negativity. Everything that doesn't serve your good—it's time to let it all go. Holding onto negative experiences and bitter emotions are like toxins, slowly killing you from the inside out. Let them go.
Inhale white, healing light.
Exhale tension.
Inhale light. Exhale anxiety.
Inhale light. Exhale anger.
Inhale healing. Exhale hatred.
Inhale light. Exhale resentment.
Inhale healing. Exhale pain.
Do this for a while until you feel yourself let go of all negativity you've been holding inside.
Now, it is time to relax your body. This is crucial, because only from this completely relaxed state can you really talk to your body, send it love and gratitude, appreciate it, and encourage it to activate its healing power. Only when you are physically relaxed and have managed to calm your mind, your body can repair itself.
Breathing slowly and consciously, bring your attention to your toes and feet. Tense your feet, from your toes to your heels, then count to three—three, two, one. After you've counted, allow them to loosen. Enjoy the relief. Relax all the way up to your ankles. Then intentionally tense up the muscles of your lower legs. Hold them tensed for a moment, counting to three—three, two, one, and release. Relax your knees.
Now, bring awareness to your thighs. Feel the front and the back of your thighs. Tense the heavy thigh muscles. Count three, two, one, then allow them to relax. Allow your legs to open up to the ceiling, completely relaxed. Squeeze your glutes as tightly as you can. Hold them tensed for a moment—three, two, one, and relax them. Allow your glutes, hips, and pelvic area to relax.
Take a breath in and dedicate breathing out to even more of your lower body, relaxing it. Repeat this a few times. Feel the ease spreading throughout your lower body, making it so heavy that it sinks deeper into the surface beneath it.
Make sure your hands are lying straight down beside your body, with your palms up. Notice the sensations in your fingers. Stretch and tense them for a moment, and then let them relax. Relax your palms, hands, and wrists. It feels so good to rest your hands. They do so much work for you.
Now, move your attention up to your forearms. Tense them to the count of three, two, one, and then release them. Relax your elbows. Move up to your upper arms. Tense the muscles and hold them tight for a moment. Count three, two, one, then allow them to loosen. Your entire hands and arms are relaxed, from your fingertips to your shoulders.
Now, notice how your stomach as it goes up and down to match the rhythm of your breathing. Intentionally squeeze all your abdominal muscles and pull your navel to your spine. Hold them tensed for three, two, one, then relax, allowing your belly to get back to its natural, relaxed state.

Take a nice, deep breath and fill your chest to the full capacity, so your chest muscles are tensed. Three, two, one, then breathe out, allowing the muscles to loosen. Notice how relaxed your stomach and chest are.

Now, bring your awareness to your back and feel the surface below it, supporting it. Tense up your back muscles from the lower back to the upper back. Breathe in and hold them tight, and with your out-breath, relax your lower back. Inhale deeply again, and as you exhale, relax the middle part of your back. Move your attention to your upper back, breathe in, and with your next exhale, relax your upper back. Feel how loosened and relaxed your back is, as if you've just gotten a massage. Allow your back to sink further down into the surface beneath it. Feel how light you are, as if you are floating yet being strongly supported.

It's time to relax your shoulders now. Breathing in, tense them up as much as you can, so they're almost touching your ears. Then, with your exhale, allow them to drop and relax. Feel the muscles of your shoulders loosen, becoming elastic and soft. Continue to breathe in, and relax them more with each exhale. When you relax your shoulders, notice how your whole body relaxes. Feel the relief. It feels so good to shake off all the burdens from your shoulders and finally give them much-deserved rest.

Now, breathing in, gently push your jaw to your chest to tense up your neck. Breathing out, bring your head back and allow your neck to relax. Bring full awareness to your throat as you breathe in again. With your next exhale, allow your throat to soften and open.

Breathing in, clench your jaw once more. Breathing out, release it, allowing it to drop.

Breathing in, tense up your facial muscles by squeezing them, group by group, and then relaxing them as you breathe out. Relax your lips, your cheeks, your eye muscles. Relax your mouth and your tongue. Inhaling, tense up your scalp and your forehead by raising your eyebrows. Exhaling, let them relax. Relax the back of your head and the top of your head. Feel its weight on the surface below you, and enjoy the sensation of being cradled by the surface.

Your whole body is now completely relaxed. Feel the ease and tranquility. Breathe deeply and slowly, and enjoy these moments of deep relaxation. Your organs, systems, blood, bones, and cells are all relaxing now. They are all regenerating and healing. There's so much happening in your body right now. Appreciate these moments of deep, re-energizing rest.

How often do you take time to appreciate your body and its incredible abilities? How often do you tell it how grateful you are for having it, and for everything it does for you? It is time to tell your body how grateful you are for it, and how much you love and appreciate it.

To start, mentally thank your feet and legs for holding you up and taking you everywhere you want to go. It's such a blessing to be able to change your location by simply moving your feet.

Now, thank your glutes for supporting you while you are sitting. Mentally say "thank you" to your genitals for bringing you joy, and your reproductive organs for giving you the possibility to reproduce. Thank your urinary and digestive systems for cleaning out your body and getting rid of everything you no longer need. Moving upward, thank your stomach for digesting food for you, without any conscious effort from you, enabling you to use nutrients. Now, thank your lungs for keeping you alive by making you breathe and use oxygen. Thank your back for the support it gives you, holding you up. Thank your hands for doing so much for you—holding, bringing, taking, carrying, hugging, creating, and so much more. Thank your neck for holding up and moving your head.

Too often, we are not aware of how blessed we are to just be able to move, to breathe, to walk, to see. Acknowledge all your blessings. Feel how grateful you are from the bottom of your heart.

Your mind is a magnificent thing. It delegates all the functions in your body, manages all the activities, and rules your thinking, far better and faster than any machine. Thank your brain for doing such a spectacular job.

Thank your mouth for enabling you to express yourself, to communicate, to taste the food you eat, to kiss. Say "thank you "to your nose and eyes. It's a precious gift to be able to see. You can see colors, faces, nature. You can see the faces of people you love. Isn't that alone enough for you to be grateful for the rest of your life?

Your body needs to hear that gratitude and appreciate from you. So allow appreciation to overflow you. If you truly allow yourself to feel deep gratitude for all of your blessings, you may even experience tears of happiness.

There's no better medicine in the world than love. Love has the power to heal everything. Nothing will help your body recover more than when you show it how loved it is. Make your love and appreciation for it a regular practice using this meditation. Mentally pour love into every part of your body.

Begin from your feet again. Mentally tell them, "I love you," and focus on really feeling it. Moving up, send lots of love to your legs, your hips, your glutes. Now feel the love for your belly and chest. Your back also needs to hear, "I love you." Pour love into your hands and arms. Say "I love you" to your shoulders and neck. Then, fill your head with pure love. Mentally tell your whole body, "I love you. You are great. You do amazing things. I pour love into every part of you. Love helps you heal, and I want you to be healthy and happy." Pour love into every organ, muscle, and bone. Pour so much love into each cell as it can hold, so every cell of your body becomes a tiny star that spreads the love around it. Send so much love to your heart that your blood becomes pure love. Everything in your body is now bathing in love. Your body is full of love. Your organs work cheerfully—your heart pumps love, and the blood flows joyfully in this cheerful rhythm. You self-love is curing everything. It repairs, rejuvenates, and heals everything that needs to be fixed. If there is some part of your body that needs special attention, pour extra love into that place. Infinite and unconditional love is spreading from your heart.

You are the one who heals yourself and does it by using the most powerful cure: endless love.

Now you are deeply relaxed. Your breathing is slow and deep. Your body is full of divine, infinite, healing love. Now, you can talk to your body and it can hear you, and you can empower the process of self-healing whenever you want.

Remind your body of its natural power to heal itself and restore balance. Tell it that you trust it and its natural wisdom.

Now, it's time to tell your body everything you want. Listen to these statements and repeat them, either mentally or out loud.

*Body, I love you.*
*I pour love into you.*
*You are perfect, just the way you are.*
*You deserve to be perfectly healthy.*
*Health is your inborn right.*
*You are meant to be balanced and work as a whole.*
*You can heal yourself, and you know exactly how to do that.*
*You are wise.*
*I trust you.*
*I allow you to do whatever it takes to heal.*
*You don't need help—just my trust and support, and I am giving both to you now.*
*I allow divine power to guide me and to restore you to your natural state of harmony.*
*I listen to you, I understand you, and I appreciate what you have to tell me. I know you do that because you need my attention.*
*I let go of everything that stands in the way to my healing.*
*I'm ready to let go of any negative emotions, limiting beliefs, and holding onto anything toxic.*

*You know the way, and I trust you.*
*I believe I can heal myself. I can heal every cell and every organ within me.*
*I love you. You are amazing and deserve to be completely healthy and happy.*
*I know you have everything you need for healing, and you will heal perfectly, in the way that is best for you.*

Now, visualize a massive golden gate in front of you. You push it gently and it opens, revealing a beautiful garden. You step into the garden. There's so much green—trees, flowers, and grass. The silence in the garden seems magical. You can hear only birds in the trees and insects in the grass.

The sunlight is shining through the shade of the trees. As you step down the path, you can hear the soft trickling sound of water. There still no water in sight, but you can hear it. You go further down the path in the direction of that gentle sound.

This garden is large. Finally, a marble pergola arises in front of you, and you discover that's where the sound is coming from. Coming closer, you can see a pool there. The water is sparkling and crystal-clear. You know that this water is healing water, which helps the body to remind itself of its self-healing power. You sit on the side of the pool, putting your feet in the water. To your surprise, your feet start shining. You decide to get fully into the water. The water is only waist-deep at this side of the pool. You look down at your legs, and you can see they are glimmering. You feel as though the water is massaging your feet, legs, and hips. With each step forward, the water goes a bit deeper. You are moving on, enjoying the feeling, and knowing that healing in your body is happening right now. Finally, you dive in and feel the water wrapping you like a luscious warm blanket. The water shimmers above your head, and your whole body is now sparkling with its glimmering shine.

Getting out of the water, you feel renewed and refreshed, as if the water washed away everything you needed to shake off.

Your body is now reminded of its powers and abilities to heal. It's full of energy and strength. You know that the healing process is underway within you.

Beside the pergola, you notice an outdoor daybed with a canopy. You know it's here for you. So you lie down on the daybed and make yourself comfortable. You can feel a soft breeze on your skin and the comfort of the mattress. You can hear the water trickle and smell the fresh grass.

Your whole body is now relaxed, rejuvenated, and full of fresh energy. You breathe deeply, knowing that a new part of the healing process is about to begin.

Take a deep breath in and imagine a healing, golden light entering your feet. As you breathe out, notice how your feet are shining brightly.

Breathe in again and feel the light enter the muscles and bones of your lower legs. Breathe out, and visualize your legs shining with golden light. Breathe in the light to your upper legs, allowing it to fill your thighs and hips. Your hips and whole legs are aglow with golden light. On your next inhale, fill the light entering your pelvic area, and on your exhale, see the bright light radiating from your glutes and pelvis. Breathing in, see the healing light fill your stomach. Breathing out, see the bright light spreading up from your center.

Now, inhale the healing light and feel it fill your chest. Exhale, and see your chest shine.

Breathe in the golden light through your spine and allow it to spread all over your back. Feel the golden light enter every muscle of your back. Breathe out, and see how your back glows with the light. It seems as if you are lying on a star.

Breathing in, imagine the light entering your fingers and spreading through your hands. The golden light is filling your lower and upper arms. Breathing out, notice your arms and hands shining gold.

The golden light now moves up to your shoulders, and they begin to shine. With your next breath in, your neck and head are now filling with the healing, golden light. Exhaling, notice how your head is shining brightly.

The light now moves through your skin, wraps around your organs, penetrates all bones and muscle tissues. It moves through your cells, and they bathe in the golden, healing light.

While your body is healing in the golden light, using divine wisdom and its natural powers to heal, you can empower it by sending love, blessings, and supportive thoughts. To build perfect health and achieve balance, you need to adopt new thinking patterns. To do that, repeat these affirmations below mentally or out loud. These affirmations will become your new beliefs and help you create a supportive environment for healing.

*I have the power to heal.*
*I am strong and powerful.*
*My body and mind are healing now.*
*I deserve to be perfectly healthy. That is my natural right.*
*I am ready to forgive and let go.*
*Life is supporting me.*
*The Universe has my back.*
*I love myself unconditionally.*
*I choose health.*
*I am full of energy.*
*All my cells are healthy and vibrant.*
*I am grateful for my body and its wisdom.*
*I am thankful for my positive, healthy thoughts.*
*I am grateful for the perfect balance of my body and mind.*
*I am complete.*
*I am whole.*
*I feel great and am full of energy.*
*I allow my body and mind to heal.*
*I love life, and life loves me back. It has a lot to give me, and I am ready to experience it.*
*I am in perfect harmony and at peace with the world. I allow divine energy and higher intelligence to guide my body and heal it.*

Take a nice, deep breath. Breathe out slowly.

When you're ready, gently open your eyes. You can move on with your daily activities, feeling fresh and re-energized. Or, if you want, let yourself drift off to sleep and have nice dreams.

# Guided Meditation for Self-Healing While Sleeping

Welcome to the meditation for self-healing. Whether you're not feeling well, have a diagnosis, or if you suffer from chronic pain, this meditation will help you harness the ability of your body to heal itself. During this meditation, you'll be talked into a relaxed state. From that state, you can talk to your body, send love to it, and empower it to heal.

This meditation is aimed to empower the self-healing abilities of your body while you are asleep. If you fall asleep during the meditation, your subconscious mind will listen to my words and help your body in its self-healing.

To begin, prepare for bed as usual. Find a comfy position in bed, and let this meditation lull you to sleep while your body recovers and re-energizes itself.

Slowly calm yourself before this healing journey begins. Let's do a short breathing exercise. Breathe through your nose, counting to six—one, two, three, four, five, six. Then, exhale through your mouth to the count of ten—one, two, three, four, five, six, seven, eight, nine, ten. If you can't reach those numbers as you breathe, don't be concerned in any way. Do what is convenient for you.

Repeat this sequence for a short while. And then, let yourself flow into your natural breathing pattern. While inhaling, imagine you are breathing in a beautiful, glittering light. While exhaling, imagine you are threating out all worries and negativity. Feel how your body grows more and more relaxed with each exhale.

Imagine you are lying in a beautiful, green garden full of colorful flowers. You're listening to insects in the grass, the birds in the trees, and wind whistling above you. Feel the peace and serenity of this garden.

Now, we'll relax the whole body. Breathe slowly and deeply. First, concentrate on your feet. Relax your feet. Relax your toes, heels, and all of your feet. Then relax your ankles and lower legs. Feel the entire length of your legs relaxing, from your knees to your thighs. Bring your focus to your thighs—both the front and the back of your thighs. Feel how your thighs relax more and more with each exhale. Your toes, heels, and feet are now deeply relaxed. Your ankles, lower legs, knees, and thighs are now deeply relaxed.

Focus your attention on your hips, glutes, and pelvic area. Relax your glutes and observe how, with every breath, your glutes and hips become more relaxed. And, with them, the whole lower half of your body also relaxes.

Bring your awareness to your hands. Relax your fingers and palms. Relax your wrists. Relax your forearms, then your elbows and upper arms. Your palms and fingers—relaxed. Your wrists—relaxed. Your forearms, elbows, and upper arms—all of them are relaxed.

Bring your attention to your stomach and chest. Observe how easily they move in the rhythm of your breathing. Relax your chest completely. Relax your stomach completely. Focus on your lower back, and relax your lower back. Feel the surface under your back, and relax your back, part by part, from your lower back and then slowly moving up to your shoulders.

Feel the peace within you and around you. Feel how your body is giving you thanks for this moment. There is so much good happening right now!

Now, relax your shoulders. The most crucial part of whole-body relaxation is the shoulders. Relax them and let them loosen. Observe how they relax more and more with every exhale. Notice how, by relaxing the shoulders, you loosen your whole body. Feel the relief.

Relax your neck. Relax the top of your head. Relax your forehead. Relax your ears. Relax your cheeks. Relax your lips, and let your jaw hang loose. Soften your eyes. Relax your eye muscles completely.

Breathe deeply and feel the peace. Your body is fully relaxed now.

Now, imagine a small white cloud above you. It's a beautiful cloud, and it's here only for you. It brings you healing. The cloud is right above your head. Are you excited? Do you feel happy about what the cloud brings you?

It's beginning to rain from the cloud. It's a rain of light. Feel the drops on your face. It's a healing rain. You can imagine it as you want—whether it's a light, small crystals, or pure water. Connect it with healing.

Your whole head is shining now in healing light. Enjoy it. You know what's going on now. The cloud moves down, above your neck. The raindrops fall over your neck. It starts shining too. Now, both your head and the neck shine.

The cloud moves down, and it's now above your shoulders, chest, and stomach. Feel the soft, warm rain of light. Feel the healing. Watch yourself glowing—your head, neck, shoulders, chest, and stomach.

The cloud expands above your arms. Your arms and hands begin to shine. The cloud grows more, and now it's above your hips, pelvis, glutes, and genitals. These parts are now shining in the healing light. Your head, neck, shoulders, chest, stomach, arms, legs, hips, and glutes are all shining in the healing rain. The cloud moves down, and healing raindrops are falling over your legs. Observe how your legs begin to glow. Do you feel the rain? Can you feel how it serves you and its healing purpose?

The white healing cloud is now above your whole body, and it's the same size as your whole body. It rains over your body, and all your body parts are shining. It's a rain of light, rain of health, and you shine brightly.

Say thanks to this moment. Feel grateful for the healing that's happening in you right now. If you have any health challenges, you can now bring your little white cloud above the part that needs healing. If you don't have any particular health issue, let the rain fall all over your body. Visualize yourself shining brighter as you heal.

If you have brought the healing cloud above a particular part of your body, imagine that part glowing. As it shines, it begins to work perfectly. All the cells of your body are happy to restore the balance that your body needs and deserves.

Right now, you are giving an incredible gift to your body. Your body is thankful, and it is going to show you appreciation. Enjoy this feeling of healing going on inside you right now.

Any tension that remains in the body now releases itself in the light's comfort, as the light continues to spread through every cell and every atom. As the healing light rains all over your body, your skin may tingle or feel warm. You feel all the stress and pain draining away under the drops of light.

The soft rain of light is enveloping you and spreading out—warm and powerful.

Enjoy the relaxation and feeling that the rain is bringing you. Rest in it, allowing it to do its work of healing you.

You are filled with pure, loving energy. See the healing light radiating from the center of your body.

From this relaxed state, while your body is healing itself using the rain's infinite wisdom, you can send yourself loving thoughts to support the healing process. It's time to release the old negative thinking patterns that have caused disease and disruption in your body, and to adopt new thinking patterns. It's time to build perfect, vibrant health.

Listen to my voice as I repeat the positive statements below. Allow these ideas to enter your subconscious and help you build positive new patterns that create health in your body and mind.

You can repeat my words mentally or just listen to these affirmations and let them become your new beliefs.

*I am healing my body and mind.*
*I am one with life.*

*Perfect health is my birthright.*
*I forgive all those I need to forgive.*
*I forgive myself.*
*I feel growing love for myself.*
*I take care of myself because I love myself.*
*I am choosing health for my body, mind, and spirit.*
*I am grateful for my amazing body and all the wonderful things it does every day.*
*I am grateful for my healthy body and my healthy mind.*
*I am calm and strong.*
*I am completely healthy.*
*All the cells of my body are healthy and vibrant.*
*I am full of positive energy.*
*I am full of life.*
*I am loved. I am enough. I am complete.*
*I am always healing, and I feel good.*
*I am letting go of everything that doesn't serve my highest good.*
*I am letting go of fear. I am letting go of anger, blame, sorrow, guilt, jealousy, blame, and tension.*
*I am at peace. There's no need to struggle.*
*I am a wonderful expression of life.*
*I have the power within me, and it's the same power that has created me. Now, I allow that power to heal my body and mind.*
*The past has no power over me. I'm letting go of it now.*
*I am unique and magnificent.*
*I am worthy of love just because I exist.*
*I accept and appreciate myself.*
*I'm willing to heal. I deserve all the best life has to give me. I deserve to be perfectly healthy.*
*I am in perfect balance and harmony with the world. I allow divine energy to circulate throughout my body and help it use its higher intelligence to heal.*
Take a nice, deep breath and exhale, visualizing the flowers and grass around you.
Sleep well, and have sweet dreams, knowing your body is healing. Good night!

# Table Of Contents

Introduction .................................................................................................................. 33
Guided Meditation for Overthinking ........................................................................... 34
Guided Meditation for Stopping Overthinking 2 ......................................................... 37
Guided Meditation for Overcoming Anxiety ............................................................... 39
Guided Meditation for Overcoming Anxiety 2 ............................................................ 43
Guided Meditation for Panic Attack Relief .................................................................. 47
Guided Meditation for Overcoming Depression ......................................................... 50
Guided Meditation for Overcoming Insomnia ............................................................ 56

# Introduction

We live in a frantic world, often in a rush, neglecting our true nature and our souls' needs. This fact can easily make us flip out of balance. In turn, our minds cannot calm down, constantly jumping to the past or future, entirely overlooking the present. So we spend too much time in our heads, too little time in reality. We then experience different issues, such as anxiety, panic attacks, depression, or poor sleep.
Fortunately, there is an incredibly simple, natural, yet highly effective solution for all these issues. Meditation gains more and more popularity these days as people discover its many benefits.
It's almost unbelievable how much a simple practice like meditation can transform one's life, help with so many issues, and restore one back to balance.
However, meditation is not a replacement for conventional medical help. If you suffer from any mental issues, please use meditation and enjoy all its benefits, but also be sure to seek professional medical help.
**So how can meditation help with overthinking?**
Our minds are genuinely devoted workers, which is great—except when it's not. If you've ever had a situation where your mind goes into overdrive and you can't stop excessive thinking, you probably understand what I mean.
We're supposed to be masters of our minds, not their servants. But if you can't find the on/off button of your mind, you can't be its master, right? Luckily, meditation can tremendously help you become your mind's master.
Practicing meditation helps you learn to calm your mind, choose your thoughts, and finally regain control of your thinking. You'll learn how to use all the magnificent tools you already have, like your focus, imagination, and awareness. You won't let your mind drive you wherever it wants, chewing its old trash over and over again. Instead, you'll become the one who chooses and decides how to use the mind's powers.
**How can meditation help with anxiety, depression, and mental health?**
Anxiety is often a consequence of our mind being too much focused on the future, trying to solve all possible problems and scenarios before they happen. Most of our mind's fears will never come true, but meanwhile, we miss out on the present.
Not to mention how awful we feel. Our mind's fears turn on all the panic buttons in our body, putting us in fight or flight mode. If you try to solve the problem on a rational level by thinking even more about the problem, you're getting yourself in an endless spiral. Rather, the solution is on the other side—by stopping useless thinking, and focusing on physical sensations and conscious presence. Meditation is the answer.
The same goes for when you experience panic attacks. If you're having an acute anxiety or panic attack, it might be hard to remind yourself that you are not in real danger. But meditation can help you calm your body and breathing, which sends signals to your mind to calm down, thereby bringing you relief.
Meditation can also help with overcoming depression. If you suffer from depression, it will help you look at things from different perspectives and gain new insights.
Meditation is a wonderful way to reconnect with your inner self, along with rediscovering your true nature and the incredible power within you. Meditation will help you tremendously in coping with any issue and improve your overall quality of life.
The guided meditations that follow have been created to help you on this journey. Just listen to my voice, relax, enjoy the moment, and allow the process to unfold.

# Guided Meditation for Overthinking

Welcome to the guided meditation for overthinking.
Please, listen to this meditation only when you can safely bring your full awareness to your complete comfort and relaxation.
This guided meditation session is aimed at helping you finally release yourself from overthinking and create peace in your inner space. It will also help you learn to calm your mind by training it to observe more and engage less.
This meditation is designed to help you free yourself from constant, useless mental activity—that is, the tendency of your mind to be busy all the time. This practice will help you gain significant insights into the thinking patterns that don't serve you, so you can end them and experience the positive benefits of letting them go.
You've probably noticed that at times, your thoughts can build up so much that you simply can't stop them anymore. They become a constant mental chatter that causes you stress and anxiety. Our minds are used to being busy all the time with unhelpful mental activity. Your mind might have developed habits of worrying, overanalyzing, and reliving personal events over and over again. Your mind needs problems to solve, so it seeks problems no matter if they exist or not. You might feel trapped or locked in an endless spiral of thinking without the ability to stop. These thinking patterns are frequently connected to chronic anxiety and depression.
Fortunately, there is an exit from this thinking spiral and you can find relief from it. The solution isn't to think more, but the opposite: to step out of your head. Focusing on physical sensation and learning to be truly present in here and now will help you stop your unwanted thinking. Practicing mindfulness meditation will teach you how to do that.
With these simple techniques that comprise this meditation, you'll learn how to train your conscious mind to focus on more productive matters, switch from useless mental activity to enjoying present-moment sensations, be consciously present, and change your emotional responses.
Let us begin.

Choose a time in the day when you can focus solely on relaxation and won't be disturbed for a while. Find a comfortable place where you can be alone, listen, and enjoy inner silence.
Find a comfortable position and posture. You can either sit or lie down, but just be sure that nothing is drawing your attention. Your back should be straight and all your muscles in an effortlessly relaxed position.
Once you find the best posture for you, bring your attention inward. Focus on your breathing. Don't try to control or hold your breath; just observe it and be aware of each breath.
Notice everything you can about your breath. Notice the cool air entering your nostrils and going down, through your airways, to your lungs and stomach. Notice your stomach and chest rise and fall in the rhythm of your breathing. Become aware of all the muscles engaging that help your chest and stomach rise and fall. Become aware of your ribs expanding and contracting with each breath. Feel the air coming all the way back to your nose and out. No need to control your breath or change anything; just breathe in your natural rhythm and observe, letting go of the need to control.
Now, become aware of the temperature of your body. Notice any warmth and coolness. Some parts of your body might be warmer than others, and some parts of your body may be cooler than others. That's normal for all resting bodies.

Acknowledge any sensations of warmth or coolness in your hands and fingers. Notice the warmth or coolness in your feet and toes. Notice any sensations of warmth or coolness in your legs and arms. Notice any sensations of warmth or coolness in the center of your body.

Just become aware of these sensations and acknowledge that they're perfectly normal. Accept them and allow yourself to stay with them for a moment.

As your body relaxes, you might notice some movements. Acknowledge those movements without forcing your body to be totally still. Become aware of all the movements of the body. Notice that some parts may feel more relaxed than others, while others may feel tension or tightness. And that's alright. You don't have to force any relaxation. For now, it's enough to acknowledge those sensations. Just allow your mind to observe and accept everything for what it is. You don't have to do a thing. You don't have to think or control anything.

Allow yourself to be at your normal pace. You don't have to rush anywhere. You are at the right place, at the right time. You don't need to be anywhere else. This is time just for you, for your relaxation and for gaining a better self-understanding.

Meditation will help you learn about yourself and get to know yourself better. You'll better understand your reactions, behaviors, and you'll grow the ability just to observe and accept things for what they are. You will learn to be fully aware and present in every moment.

As you continue to breathe consciously, you are fully present in the here and now.

If you want, you can slow your breathing now. Allow your next in-breath to be just a little slower and your next out-breath to be just a little longer.

By slowing your cycles of breathing, you're sending signals to your mind to slow down. As your mind receives that feedback, your body and mind alike continue to gently slow.

It feels so good to calm your mind. Notice you don't have any excessive thoughts. You are not using much thinking energy. You are simply thinking in a normal manner and naturally asking your body to slow down and calm its breathing.

Notice your slow breathing. It's so easy and effortless. As you bring your focus to your breathing, you feel deeply relaxed and fully present.

As you observe each breath with a clear space in your mind, you notice every thought that arises. Just observe each thought that your mind wishes to create. These thoughts might be internal judgments, evaluations, labels, phrases, words, or images—any kind of distractions. Sometimes your thought may be a description.

Your mind is not used to being quiet. It has a need to do something, or at least, to describe or name things. Just note whatever it is that your mind wants to create. Become aware of the temporary nature of thinking.

Thoughts come and thoughts go.

You always have a choice: to follow your thoughts, or let them go. Instead of following your thoughts, choose to remain a little further removed from them. By doing so, you are allowing yourself to stay outside of your mind's evaluations and judgments. Instead, you allow yourself to simply be, by simply noticing these creations of the mind.

So allow any thought that arises to just exist there. There is no need to try to control thinking. There's no need to try to change thoughts or thinking. Simply acknowledge the thoughts, allow them to be there for a while, and give them space to play.

When you give up trying to control your thoughts, acceptance and allowance will make such thoughts come and go whenever they want, and the thoughts will eventually fade away.

Yes, those thoughts are yours. But you also know and understand that who you are is much more than just your thoughts.

You witness the sparks of thoughts come and go, almost like shooting stars across a clear night sky. As a single thought comes into your mind, you easily notice how it carries its own certain energy. Some thoughts have particularly strong energy and call for attention. Others are quieter.

But you can always stay outside all your thoughts by observing, resting, and relaxing.

From a comfortable distance, you can witness and watch as each thought arises and simply passes. As you are calm and observant in each moment, you can choose to turn your focus and awareness inwards back to your breathing—breathing in and breathing out. You are always able to return to this focus on your breath.

Now, allow your awareness to note and observe small sensations that come with each breath. In this way, you are training your observant mind. So notice the cool air as it enters your nostrils, passes through your nose, and becomes slightly warmer as it moves down through your airways. Feel it enter your lungs. There's no need to hold your breath. Just remain mindful and observe your natural breathing cycles, allowing your body to breathe deeply and completely in its natural rhythm. Don't try to control your breathing. Just silently observe each breath.

This technique is known as mindful breath awareness, and it is a powerful technique. By allowing yourself to focus on breathing in this simple way, you can gently guide and return your conscious awareness back to your breath.

And as you allow individual thoughts to enter your awareness—wherever or whenever they arise—you offer them your calmest acknowledgement. You allow them to pass by, and their energy fades, burns out, or disappears. You let thoughts pass by, offering no resistance.

By using this technique, you can observe who you really are. You are so much more than your thoughts. You're observing, and calmly detaching yourself. By calming yourself, you always remain in the present moment.

You are gaining the understanding that you are more than your thinking and your reactions. There's always one more part of you that is always observing, watching, and witnessing. You are easily able to return to your breath as often as you need. You can always make a choice to remain present in the moment by coming back to your breath, breathing in and breathing out.

You are consciously present now. Your mind is peaceful now.

You can remain in this mindful state for as long as you wish.

If you wish, you can drift off to sleep from here. Or you may choose to remain awake and alert, calmly observing your breathing for as long as you want.

When you are ready, slowly open your eyes, get up, and go on with your usual activities, aware that you can always come back to this state of complete mindfulness.

# Guided Meditation for Stopping Overthinking 2

Welcome to the guided meditation that will help you stop excessive thinking. Feel free to use this meditation whenever you feel the need to reach a state of peace without excessive thoughts. This meditation will have you find mental calm.

Make yourself comfortable in a sitting or lying position. For a better experience, I recommend that you listen to this meditation with earphones.

Breathe deeply, focusing particularly on your exhales.

Bring awareness to your breathing. Feel more relaxed with each exhale. Breathe deeply in and out, using your stomach.

Bring attention to your feet. Relax your feet.

Relax your toes, heels, and your whole feet.

Relax your ankles. Feel the relaxed sensation in your ankles.

Focus on your lower legs and intentionally relax them. Relax the front and the backside of your lower legs. Completely relax every part of your legs.

Continue to breathe deeply, focusing on your out-breaths.

Relax your knees. Relax your thighs, both the front and the backside of your thighs.

Notice that your toes, heels, and feet are relaxed. Your ankles—relaxed. Your lower legs, knees, and upper legs—relaxed.

Bring awareness to your glutes and your hips. Relax every part of them. Feel the whole lower half of the body relax. With every exhale, your glutes relax further.

Now, concentrate on your palms and hands. Relax your hands. Let your fingers relax. Relax your wrists. Continue to breathe deeply, concentrating on your exhales.

Relax your arms, allowing your elbows to loosen. Relax your upper arms. Your fingers, palms, wrists, whole hands—relax all of them. Your lower arms, elbows, and upper arms—relax all of them.

Now, bring awareness to your stomach and chest. Breathing deeply, relax your stomach and chest.

Now, concentrate on your lower back. Feel all the muscles of your lower back. Relax your lower back and let this relaxed sensation move upwards to your shoulders.

Allow your shoulders to relax and feel the relief. With each out-breath, your shoulders relax even. Even when you think you have relaxed them completely, you can still relax them a bit more.

Observe how your whole body is more relaxed as you continue to relax your shoulders.

Now, let your neck relax. Relax the back of your head. Allow your cheeks and forehead to relax. Relax your ears.

Relax your mouth and jaw, letting your jaw fall loose. Relax and soften your eyes. Relax all those tiny eye muscles.

As you relax, notice your thoughts. It's normal to have thoughts. It's natural. Don't resist them and don't try to fight them. Just acknowledge them and choose which of them you want to engage.

The main purpose of this meditation is to create your safe place, your peaceful room, where you can enter whenever you want to rest and calm your mind.

Imagine your mind as a house with rooms in it. You have separate rooms for work, for family, for health, for relationships, for finances, and for love. You have a room for each segment of your life.

Also, imagine you have rooms for your worries and problems. Now, enter one of those rooms. You find that it's loud, full of thoughts and worries. As you stand in that room, observe which thoughts are in there. Observe them, listen to them. As you do, you notice one thing: those are not your thoughts. These thoughts belong to the room that you have entered. How do you feel while watching and listening to the thoughts in this room? Which emotions do they provoke? Do you feel worried, stressed, or frightened?

Now, exit that room and go to your room. This room is pure white. It's a room without thoughts. You see yourself entering that room—white, bright, clean, and airy. Open the door and enter the peaceful space. There's nothing else. It's absolutely quiet there.

Observe your body now.

Observe the peace you feel in that white room. This room is your safe place from now on.

Stay in the room for a while, absolutely conscious. You are aware that this room is the room without any thoughts. Acknowledge the peace and silence in this room. There's nothing but pure existence here.

Peace. Calm. Serenity.

Now, once more, intentionally enter one of the other rooms that are full of thoughts. Choose the worst room, the one with the loudest worries, the most negative thoughts, and the problems that bother you most.

As you stand in that room, observe those thoughts. Watch them.

Now, you feel differently because you know now you can exit this room whenever you want.

Once more, go again to your safe room—the white and quiet room. Once you open that door, feel the silence and peace. There are no thoughts here, just absolute peace.

Now, you know there are many rooms in your mind. But there's always one safe room where you can enter, rest, and be at peace. Go to this room whenever you feel you want to rest from your thoughts. If sometimes you find yourself in loud, negative thinking, don't fight it or blame yourself, just be aware you have entered a room full of thoughts. So remind yourself that you can always exit that loud, unpleasant room and go to your safe and peaceful room.

Now, stay in your safe room. Look around. For the first time, you realize that you can actually see the peace and hear the silence in this room. Acknowledge that this is a space without thoughts. You have the power to choose to be there—in this room—whenever you want.

# Guided Meditation for Overcoming Anxiety

Welcome to the guided meditation for releasing anxiety. It is aimed at helping you calm your mind and find relief from excess worries and chronic stress.

Suffering from anxiety can be overwhelming at times. This meditation will help you reduce it and eventually set yourself free from it.

Before you start the meditation, choose a time of the day when you know you won't be disturbed for about half an hour and find a silent place where you can be alone.

Take time to make yourself comfortable, lying on your back, if possible, with your hands relaxed next to the body and legs straight, relaxed, and slightly opened.

Once you find a comfortable posture, I invite you to listen to my guidance. This meditation session will teach you how to find relief and find a place of inner peace whenever you need it.

This is the time to rest your mind and body from anxiety. You are safe now, and you can observe your anxiety from a safe distance. It's safe to relax now, and it's safe to look from this place at all the thoughts that provoke your anxiety.

Now, let your body and mind relax. Allow yourself to release all the tension and disturbing thoughts, and experience a sense of deep peace.

Now, give your thoughts permission to rest. You don't need them right now. This is the time for rest from thinking or doing anything else. There's nothing to be worried about. You are safe now, in a place of complete serenity.

Most often, anxiety occurs because we are too much in our heads and too little in the physical world. Also, we are constantly focusing on the future and the things that might happen. Most of those things never happen, except in our heads. The only reality that exists for us is this moment, here and now. And if you pay attention, you'll notice that at this moment, all is well. So this meditation practice will help you learn how to ground yourself and become truly present in this moment.

It's safe to pause, rest, and relax now. Things have their natural rhythm, and all will be well. You'll be fine, and the anxiety will pass. You won't feel tension forever. You just need to learn how to let it go.

Know that you're in the right place, doing the right thing. There's no need to be anywhere else. There is nothing else you should be doing right now.

Your natural state of being is calm and relaxed. There's nothing wrong with you if you have trouble reaching this natural state – you just need to remind yourself to get back into balance. The key is never to think more. You can't find relief by producing more mental activity. The solution is to calm your mind and be present.

Now, bring your undivided attention to this moment. Don't try to solve anything in your mind. Just let your thoughts pass by.

Bring attention to your body. Notice how it feels. Notice if you feel particular tension in some parts. Focus on each body part and notice exactly how it feels. Doing this, you're already making the first step towards relief and stepping out of your head.

Anxiety is undoubtedly unpleasant. But it's not dangerous as it seems. You are safe. You are stronger than what's bothering you. You are more than your thoughts and stronger than your fears.

Keep your attention on your body. Scan your body, devoting undivided attention to each part and relaxing it.

Notice the most tensed areas of your body, where you are holding the most stress and anxiety. Give some extra love and attention to those parts, trying to relax them as much as possible. Breathe deeply, and with every exhale, try to relax those parts a bit more.

Start focusing on your toes. Focus on them and intentionally relax them. Now, relax your whole feet. Let your ankles relax. Allow this relaxed feeling to move upwards to your legs. Let your knees relax. Loosen your thighs. Allow your hips and glutes to relax. Notice the entire lower half of the body relaxing more and more.

Notice if there's still any tension remaining somewhere in your lower body. If there's any part still holding the anxiety, remember it. You'll come back to those parts later.

Now, invite your attention to your stomach and chest. Notice how relaxed your stomach and chest are as they rise and fall with your breathing. Allow your chest muscles to relax. Feel how your ribcage is floating.

Feel the press of the surface beneath your back. Imagine you are breathing in through your spine. Then, start to relax your back muscles from the lowest point upward, part by part. With each exhale, relax your back muscles a bit more.

Once you reach your shoulders, take a deep breath and exhale, now relaxing your whole back.

If you notice some parts of your back are still tensed, make a mental note.

Now, focus on your fingers. Allow all of them to relax. Allow your palms to relax, and notice how your hands open up toward the ceiling. Relax every part of your hands. Then allow that relaxed sensation to move up to your arms.

Now, we come to a crucial part of relaxation—your shoulders. Your shoulders are where we hold and carry most of our anxiety, worries, stress, and fears. Most often, our shoulders are constantly tensed while we are not even aware of that tension.

So focus on your shoulders. Feel all the tension and weight you've been carrying in them. If you are used to keeping your shoulders tensed all the time, it might be difficult to relax them. Just be patient and do your best. Breathe in. Breathe out, allowing your shoulders to drop down. Do it again--breathe in, then breathe out through your mouth, allowing all the tension and anxiety to fall from your shoulders. Let go of all the weight, all the worries, stress, and anxiety. Breathe in. Breathe out, and relax your shoulders a bit more. Even when you think your shoulders are completely relaxed, there's still space to relax them more. Breathe in. Breathe out, and allow your shoulders to relax even more. Notice how nice it feels to relax your shoulders. It's like getting a relaxing massage. Notice how your whole body relaxes even more as you relax your shoulders.

Now, let your neck relax. Allow your throat to open up and relax, and the back of your neck to soften.

Notice if there's any part of your neck still tensed, and make a note if so.

Make a conscious effort to relax your ears and the back of your head. Feel the weight of your head on the surface below. Relax your facial muscles. Relax your mouth. Allow the jaw to relax and drop down. Relax your tongue. Don't worry about how you look right now. Relax your cheeks. There's no need for any tension in your face. Our faces are often tensed all day long as we play our social roles.

Relax all of your face now. Allow your forehead and eyebrows to relax. Relax all those tiny muscles around your eyes. Calm your eyes and allow them to relax in your head. Notice how good it feels to calm your eyes. Relax the top of your head.

Take a nice, deep breath, and with your exhale, relax your whole body once again.

Once again, scan the whole body with your complete awareness. Notice all those parts that still hold anxiety and tension. Tension might still be lingering in your shoulders, jaw, cheeks, forehead, scalp, or anywhere else in your body. Check everything and notice where you still feel any tension.

Now, visualize a feeling of warmth in those parts. It's a pleasant warmth, not too strong. Visualize that your body is made of chocolate. Your tensed parts are slowly warming up. Then, they begin to melt. It feels so good to melt those parts. They become relaxed, elastic, and soft. There's no stress, tension, or anxiety in those parts anymore.

Enjoy this relaxed feeling, visualizing the smell of warm chocolate. Your body feels like it's being massaged from the inside by your undivided attention.

Now, turn your attention inward again and scan the whole body—notice which part is the most relaxed. Now, visualize this part as a spot of intense, pleasant warmth. This warmth is now spreading through your body in all directions. The zone of warmth grows, spreading relaxation through the whole body. This pleasant warmth fills the whole body until it pushes out even the tiniest pieces of anxiety.

Your whole body is now warm and relaxed. There's nothing else you should be doing right now but enjoying this relaxation and rest. This is your gift to yourself.

Now, focus on your breathing. Our breath is the simplest, yet most powerful thing which keeps us alive. It's also your most powerful cure for anxiety. It can help you calm down, bring your attention to your physical existence, and relax your mind. No thought or fear can survive while you're consciously breathing. Just concentrating on your breathing is enough.

Thoughts will come, for sure, but thoughts will also go. You don't need to fight them. All you need to do is bring your focus back to your breath.

Continue to observe your breathing. Notice everything you can about it. Feel the air entering your nostrils, going down your airways, filling your lungs, and going all the way back out as you exhale. Place your hands on your stomach and feel how your stomach expands as you draw air in. Imagine the emptiness and feel the way of the air leaving your body as you exhale.

Stay with your breath. If you start to feel anxiety, just take another deep breath and focus on the sensation of air filling your lungs.

Breathe in, counting to four—one, two, three, four.

Then, holding your breath, counting to three—one, two, three.

Exhale, counting to eight—one, two, three, four, five, six, seven, eight.

Once again, inhale, counting to four—one, two, three, four.

Holding your breath, count to three—o ne, two, three.

Exhale, counting to eight—one, two, three, four, five, six, seven, eight.

If some thought distracts you, just notice it and let it go. Bring your attention back to your breathing.

Imagine the air you inhale is pure peace and calmness, and the air you exhale is your anxiety. Every time you exhale, you're letting go of tension and anxiety. You're changing it for peace and relaxation.

Feel how the relaxed space becomes bigger and bigger, and the space filled with anxiety shrinks and becomes smaller until it completely disappears. Notice how your breathing soothes and calms you.

Now, while inhaling, mentally say to yourself: "Relax." While you're exhaling, repeat: "Relax."

Once again: inhale—relax, exhale—relax.

Your body is relaxed and your mind is calm. Thoughts are slowing down. You are safe now. Stay calm and feel in control.

Now, in this safe environment, think about how you feel when you are overflowed with anxiety. Tell yourself it's normal to feel that way. The next time you feel that way, remind yourself it's okay and it will pass.

Now, let your mind relax. You don't have to focus on anything anymore. Just rest, relax, and trust everything will be fine.

You are at a special place now. This is the place of inner peace and serenity. There are no worries here. All is well. Not only do you feel relief, but you have also learned how to get to this special place. Just your breath and your focus have brought you here. This is the place within you, and you can get there whenever you want. Here, you can always find shelter and relief from worries and anxiety, even in the middle of the day.

You can stay with this feeling even when you finish with the meditation. This peace can stay with you throughout your usual daily activities.

So the next time you start to feel anxiety, you might simply remember this meditation, and it might be enough to ground you in peace. You'll be able to release anxiety and take back control, breathing deeply, relaxing, and bringing yourself to the present moment.

By practicing this meditation, you'll become more and more confident. You'll know that you are bigger than anything that causes your anxiety.

You are strong. You are calm. You are free. You are peaceful. You are powerful. You are hopeful. You are positive. You are serene.

For those of you who want to go on with your daily activities now that the meditation is over, it's time to wake up. Slowly move your hands and toes, and gently stretch your body. When you feel ready, open your eyes. This peace will stay with you throughout your day.

For those of you who want to fall asleep after the meditation: just go on and enjoy the relaxed feeling that will lull you to sleep. When you wake up, you'll be refreshed and renewed, calm, and relaxed. Sleep well, and have nice dreams.

# Guided Meditation for Overcoming Anxiety 2

Welcome to the second guided meditation for relieving anxiety. It has been created to help you change anxiety for balance and inner peace. Through this meditation practice, you'll learn how to detach yourself from disturbing thoughts and emotions, and find serenity.

Before we start, find the most comfortable position and posture. You might want to lie on your back or side, or perhaps you'd like to sit. Whatever you choose, it's okay. Also, don't force yourself to be still—feel free to move during the meditation if you want to. Just follow your gut and make yourself comfortable.

This is time only for you. Everyone needs some time to themselves, to calm their mind and sort through their thoughts. Enjoy this time for rest and recharge—it's a simple, pleasant, yet incredibly powerful cure for anxiety.

Suffering from anxiety often means your mind is hyperactive, crazy busy, and focused on the future. You have rushing thoughts, which make you feel you are in trouble all the time. As if there's always some problem you should be solving or a danger you should run from or fight. These thoughts make you tense and mentally absent. Meanwhile, you pay too little attention to sensations in your body and neglect your breathing. Perhaps your breath is short and shallow, as if you were in real and constant danger.

It would be so nice to have a turn-off button for anxiety, but you can't find it in your mind. Fortunately, there is a button: it is in relaxing your body. When you are tensed, your mind sends signals to the body to prepare for fight or flight. This works in the opposite direction as well. So if you manage to relax your body and calm your breathing, your mind will receive signals to slow down and relax.

Practicing this meditation, you'll learn how to relax your body, deepen your breathing, and slow your mind. That way, your brain will realize you are safe and it will switch off the panic button, stopping your anxiety.

We'll also repeat some mantras to help you remove subconscious blockages and change your beliefs about anxiety.

Now, I invite you to close your eyes and follow my voice. Bring your attention to this very moment.

Become aware of your head and try to contract the tiny muscles of your scalp and forehead. Then relax them. Relax your ears. Feel all the tension in and around your eyes. Then calm that tension, rest, and completely relax. Relax all the muscles of your face. Compress your lips, then let them relax. Clench your jaw, then let it loosen. Tense the muscles of the back of your neck by pressing the chin against the chest. Then bring your head back and relax your neck.

Contract your shoulder muscles and relax them, letting the shoulders drop down in a relaxed position. Contract your back muscles, then relax them, feeling how they loosen, one by one, until your whole back is relaxed. Fill your chest with air, and while you exhale, feel the muscles of your chest relaxing.

Pull your navel to your spine, and feel the abdominal muscles tense. Then let your stomach and all those abdominal muscles relax.

Clench your fists, contracting your hands and arms. Then release, relaxing your fingers, palms, wrists, and arms.

Contract your glutes, then slowly relax them. Notice how relaxed the whole body feels when you relax your glutes.

Contract your entire legs, from your hips to thighs, down to your feet and toes. Then relax your hips, relax your thighs, and relax your knees. Relax your ankles, and relax your feet.

Now your whole body is relaxed.

Now, bring awareness to your breathing. You don't have to change anything—just notice how you breathe in and breathe out.

Visualize yourself lying on the grass. It's a beautiful sunny day. There's a clear sky above you. Take a nice, deep breath, and as you're exhaling, imagine you are making soap bubbles. The anxiety from all parts of your body leaves you, filling these bubbles. Then visualize a bubble flying into the sky and popping, releasing your anxiety.

Inhale again, taking all the anxiety you can find, and imagine blowing it into a bubble. Then send it up into the sky. The bubble flies up, up, up, and pops.

Do this once again. Take a breath, letting your stomach expand. Then breathe out all your anxiety, making a lot of bubbles. They fly around you and upward in all directions, taking your anxiety far away. You can see them popping and disappearing.

With your next breath, collect all the anxiety you might still be holding and exhale, making a lot of bubbles. Watch the bubbles fly away.

Now, listen to the affirmations I say and slowly repeat them, mentally or out loud. Dedicate one breath to each of these affirmations.

Inhale, and repeat this mantra as you exhale. *I'm aware of my breathing. I'm aware of the air going in and out of my body.*

Inhale. Exhale, and repeat this mantra. *I'm aware of my body. I'm aware of my heart rhythm.*

Between each of mantra, focus on your inhale and exhale.

*I'm aware of my fears and anxiety. I'm aware of the discomfort I feel.*

*I'm aware of the negative thoughts that make me feel anxious.*

*Now, as I inhale and exhale, I'm slowly calming my mind.*

*I'm letting go of negative thoughts.*

*As I breathe, I'm calming my anxiety.*

*I'm relaxing my body and slowing down my thoughts.*

*With each exhale, I'm letting go of fears and concerns.*

*With each inhale, I'm finding more peace.*

*I inhale calmness. I exhale peace.*

Now, smile while you're breathing.

*Being aware of my breathing, I'm letting go of everything that doesn't serve me.*

*I inhale serenity. I exhale joy.*

*I am safe and secure. I give myself permission to be in peace.*

*I am well.*

*Things are getting better and better every day.*

*I expect great things to happen.*

Now, tell your anxiety: *I see you. It's okay. I accept you and love you.*

*I accept all my emotions. I allow myself to experience them. They don't define me. I can observe them while remaining calm.*

When you accept your emotions, instead of fighting them, they become lighter. When you set them free, they are able to flow through your body and leave you.

Say to your anxiety, "Thank you for being here to protect me. But I don't need your help anymore. I am ready to let you go now."

Notice how much lighter and freer you feel.

*I'm healing all the time. My body and mind are in healthy harmony.*

*I allow myself to be in peace.*

Now, imagine warm, golden light bathing and healing you, part by part, from your head to your toes, wrapping you in a soft glow. It's mighty, yet gentle.

*I enjoy being wrapped in a soft, warm blanket. I am safe and secure. It's so good to feel the warm, soft hug of this blanket.*

*I feel reborn and reenergized now.*

*I feel wellness in my whole body, in each cell of my body.*

*I rest in this comfort and peace. I allow myself to slip into tranquility and gentleness.*

*I enjoy being in this completely relaxed state, free from worries and anxiety.*

Now, imagine stairs that lead down. You can picture these stairs however you like. We are going downstairs.

Take a deep breath. Inhale, counting to three—one, two, three.

While exhaling, imagine you are going downstairs, counting your steps to five—one, two, three, four, five.

Inhale, counting to four—one, two, three, four.

Exhale, and move down the stairs, counting to six—one, two, three, four, five, six.

Inhale, counting to five—one, two, three, four, five.

Exhale, counting to seven—one, two, three, four, five, six, seven.

You are in a dark room now. It's not completely dark here, but you can barely see where you're going. Don't be afraid. You are safe.

Take a few steps into the room. You are in the center of the room. Imagine sitting on the floor with your legs crossed. Although it's dark in here, you can see there is an item on the floor, in front of you. It's a bowl.

You pick up the bowl and hold it in your hands. It's heavy. Its surface is smooth and cold. You can't clearly see its color, but you know it's dark.

Now, put it back on its place on the floor in front of you.

Picture your anxiety as dark sand collected in your body.

Imagine taking your anxiety, as much of it as you can grab with your hands. Put it in the bowl. Repeat this a few times.

Imagine your worries and concerns as dark, cold stones in your mind. Take them and put them into the bowl.

Repeat this action with each worry that bothers you, causing your anxiety.

Now, you've put all your anxiety, worries, and negative thoughts into the bowl.

Breathe deeply, filling your belly.

Everything is constantly changing.

Dark can turn into light.

Your worries and anxiety can change into acceptance, peace, love, power, and joy.

Notice that the bowl becomes lighter. You can clearly see the bowl now. It becomes lighter with each of your breaths. Dark sand becomes lighter too. Then, the sand starts to glow in the dark. It's a shiny powder, like glitter. The dark stones you have put into the bowl also become lighter and lighter. Now they shine brightly, like jewels. The bowl shines with bright, golden light, spreading this light all over the room. You are sitting in the bright, clean light, inhaling it.

Your thoughts have changed from dark and heavy to glimmering jewels full of luck and wonderful possibilities. As you inhale, the whole body fills with bright, healing light. Now you glow. You are peace. You are love. You are light.

When a dark thought comes to you again, you can direct it into this bowl. The bowl will turn this dark thought into light. This bowl will always be here for you.

You can come back here whenever you wish.

When you are ready, you can slowly stand up and go back to the stairs. You can take the light and your bright jewels full of positive thoughts with you.

We are going upstairs. Take a deep breath and count backward with me—six, five, four, three, two, one. You are back in your usual surroundings. But there is one significant change—you are calm and peaceful. You are spreading the light, and you know you can come back to take more of this light whenever you need.

When you feel ready, take a deep breath. Exhale, and gently open your eyes. You can go on with your activities, feeling much lighter and calmer than before.

# Guided Meditation for Panic Attack Relief

Welcome to the guided meditation for panic relief.
If you are having a panic attack right now, it's great you're here.
A panic attack can be very frightening, especially if you go through it alone, without anyone by your side. This meditation is here to support you while you're experiencing these unpleasant moments and help you get back to a state of calm.
These uneasy feelings and sensations you are having will soon pass. You might feel out of control or disconnected from your surroundings, or that something terrible will happen. You may feel that you're losing your mind or you're going to die.
But rest assured, although those sensations are very unpleasant, they will all pass. You will be okay. You are okay even now.
What you are going through is normal, although it doesn't seem so. It's a natural neurological response and cannot last for an extended period of time. It's not physically possible, because the hormones that make you feel so diminish. So this feeling will fade away.
You may already know all this, but when you're experiencing a panic attack, your survival instinct might override your rational mind. It's hard not to believe the irrational, frightening thoughts that you're having. These thoughts are all part of a fight or flight mode, and that's how our bodies and minds work. It's part of human nature—that's why it can be so hard to calm down. That's why you need reassurance that you are okay and a reminder that this will all pass. All those uncomfortable, scary, unbearable feelings you're having right now will pass.
Maybe you are also experiencing physical symptoms. Maybe you can't breathe properly, catch your breath, or maybe your heart is racing and you feel dizziness, numbness, or tingling…These sensations are all normal, and they will pass.
Let's do some calm breathing together, which will help you calm down.
Even if you feel like you can't breathe properly, you are able to breathe. It's just your mind playing tricks on you.
Say something out loud—anything. Remember, if you can talk, you can breathe.
You're probably forgetting to exhale. And that is normal when you feel endangered.
Now, visualize a lot of candles in front of you. Like on a birthday cake, for example.
Now, take a breath in, and blow out a candle.
Breathe in, slowly, through your nose. Hold it. Now, breathe out, slowly, through your mouth.
Once again--breathe in. Hold. Breathe out.
In. Hold. Out.
Everything is okay. You have enough air.
If you want, you can go on with breathing this way. Or, if you like, look around at your surroundings.
Notice everything you see.
Notice all the sounds around you.
Your anxious feelings will pass because they are not based on anything real. Your mind is playing tricks on you. You are safe, and everything is okay.
Sometimes, it can help a lot during a panic attack to drink a cold glass of water. Or, if it's nighttime, you can turn off the lights. It can also help to wash your face with cool water.
Looking through a window, counting all trees or roofs in sight can also help you distract yourself from these unpleasant bodily sensations.

Maybe none of these actions will help you right now. And that's okay, because even if you do absolutely nothing, this feeling will pass.

You don't have to do anything at all. You don't have to think, focus, or talk. We can just wait together for this feeling to fade away. Just listen to my voice, if it helps.

This unpleasant feeling will get smaller and smaller until it disappears, I promise. You will be calm again. Now, look around and notice your surroundings. Notice the colors, the light, and the textures of your surroundings. Listen to the sounds you hear. Notice your body's weight against the surface below you, or the feeling of your feet against the surface.

You are okay, even though you don't feel okay right now.

Maybe you feel a bit disconnected from your body right now. Let's do a grounding technique that will help you feel connected with your body again.

To start, squeeze your hands into fists, and tighten the muscles of your arms. Feel the tension building in your shoulders, arms, and hands. Hold them tensed for a moment. Then, let them loosen. Feel the weight of your arms as they relax. Allow your shoulders to drop.

Take a deep breath in, hold it in, and breathe out through your mouth.

Let's squeeze these body parts again, but this time, include your face. Squeeze your hands, arms, and shoulders, and crunch up all your face muscles. Squeeze them tighter and tighter. Hold for a moment. Now relax. Let your shoulders soften, and let your arms and hands relax. Allow your face to relax.

Rub your hands together, then gently place them over your eyes. Feel the warmth radiating from your palms. Notice the sensation of warm palms over your cheeks.

Now, bring your hands back into their relaxed position.

Breathe in. Hold it in. Breathe out deeply, as if you're blowing candles.

Maybe you notice your anxiety starting to fade. If not, that's okay. Sometimes, it requires more time. Simply accepting a panic attack and anxiety for what they are and not trying to eliminate them will help. Notice how you feel. It doesn't matter if you good or bad—just notice. Let go of all resistance.

Try to soften your body as much as you can. Are there areas that are extra-tensed—your throat, neck, jaw, or anywhere else? Try to soften them intentionally, even if it's just a little.

Everything changes, always. This unpleasant feeling will change too. You just need to let that chnage happen. Feeling anxious is not bad. It is what it is, a physical reaction. Nothing different from the flu or any body ache. It's okay. Anxiety may be scary, but it can't hurt you.

Breathe in. Hold. Breathe out.

You are safe. Everything's okay.

Now, allow yourself to rest and allow your relaxation response to kick in.

While you do that, listen to these affirmations. Eventually, you'll begin to feel even calmer.

Take a deep breath in through your nose. Breathe out through your mouth.

Go on with breathing like this, deeply and slowly.

*I accept the way I feel right now.*
*It's okay to be anxious.*
*This anxiety will soon fade.*
*I accept how I feel at this moment.*
*I know this feeling will soon pass.*
*I accept whatever I am feeling.*
*I will not resist.*
*I'm feeling calmer and more relaxed.*
*I will be okay.*
*I am okay.*

*I am safe.*
*I already feel a bit calmer and more relaxed than a moment ago.*
*I am feeling so much more relaxed.*
*I am breathing much easier now.*
*My muscles are more relaxed.*
*My face is smooth and relaxed.*
*My throat feels open and relaxed.*
*My chest feels lighter.*
*My heart is calmer.*
*My belly is soft.*
*I am calm.*
*I am at ease.*
*My thoughts are slowing down.*
*With each passing moment, I feel better and better.*
*I know I am safe.*
*I am peaceful.*
*I am relaxed.*
*I am calm.*
*I am serene.*
*I am at ease.*
*I am peaceful, relaxed, calm, and at ease.*
*I am safe, and all is well.*

# Guided Meditation for Overcoming Depression

Welcome to this meditation designed to help you with depression and depressive moods.

During this meditation session, you'll gain a new perspective and learn a new way to look at your thoughts and feelings.

As soon as you finish this meditation, you may find you'll feel better. You'll immediately feel more hopeful.

If you regularly practice this meditation, you'll feel depressed less often. Eventually, you'll notice depression has disappeared from your life and you have your old self back again.

Yet, keep in mind that this meditation is meant to ease depression and help you during the process, but it can't replace professional help. So please, seek professional help and use this meditation as a supplement.

To begin, choose a time when you won't be disturbed and you're free to safely close your eyes, listen, and relax for a while. Remember, this quiet, "me time" is not a luxury. It's a need and will tremendously enrich your healing.

Before we begin with the meditation, take time to find a comfortable position. You can be lying or sitting. It's up to you, and everything is okay as long as your back is straight yet relaxed.

Make sure your clothes feel comfortable, and loosen all restrictive belts or pieces. Turn off any ringers and notifications.

Place your hands beside your body. Or, place them on your lap or knees, with your palms turned up.

If you wish, close your eyes. If you want to keep them open, that's okay, too.

Take a few deep and slow breaths. Connect with your breath. Observe how it affects your body. Notice all the sensations and movements connected with it. Feel the air entering your nostrils. Notice your belly rising and falling with the in-breaths and the out-breaths.

Now, allow your breathing to settle into its natural rhythm and let go of trying to control it.

Be aware of your body, its posture, its place in the space around you, and its weight on the surface beneath you.

Notice all sensations in the body. Feel all your body parts.

Remain aware of your breathing and its natural rhythm.

Depression is universal. It's part of being human. We all feel depressed from time to time. But when it lasts for a long time, it affects everything—our bodies and our health, along with our mindset, thinking, emotions, and all aspects of life. There's a whole package of negative feelings coming from depression. It can make you look at life through dark glasses, leaving you unable to see anything positive. Eventually, it seems as if all your interests have faded away.

Depression is a natural reaction to loss. However, you can also be depressed for no apparent reason. That doesn't make your depression any easier, nor does it mean anything is wrong with you. Either way, know that your thoughts and emotions are normal.

Although depression is tough and not at all fun, depression can bring you something good. It can compel you to turn inward, examine your problems and perspectives, gain meaningful insights, reevaluate things in your life, and make adjustments to your life.

Certainly, living with depression is not something you should accept as permanent. Know there is always a solution out there for it. Seek professional help and support from people around you. Use this meditation as often as you can. This meditation will teach you techniques that will help you feel better. You can use these techniques whenever you need them.

Whatever your emotions and thoughts are, you should not ignore, suppress, or deny them. Whatever you fight or deny grows stronger. So the solution is not in digging for the root of the problem and figuring out where it comes from. This is not the ways to get rid of negative thoughts and feelings. A better solution is to change your relationship with them.

Instead of resisting and fighting hard feelings, accept them, make space for them to play, and stay with them for a while. Give them your attention—your emotions are trying to tell you something. They are telling you where you are not faithful to your true self.

So when you offer your emotions acceptance instead of resistance, you'll see, much to your surprise, how they lose their power and fade away.

Now, make yourself comfortable so you can relax. If you fall asleep during the meditation, that's okay—your subconscious mind will be listening to and recording everything I say. But, if possible, try to stay alert during the session so you can consciously engage in your healing.

Breathe in and out your natural pattern. You don't need to change your rhythm or depth of breathing for now. Just breathe in your usual way.

Place your attention on your nose. Feel the air entering your nostrils. Feel the coolness of the air. Now, notice the air leaving your nostrils. Notice its warmth.

Do this for a few moments. Focus on breathing cool air in and warm air out. Concentrate only on the sensations in your nose.

Do it once again—cool air in, warm air out.

Now, explore your breath and allow yourself to experience it fully. Watch your breath and be curious. Feel the experience of breathing, and observe yourself having that experiecnce at the same time.

If your natural breathing is long and deep, notice that. If your normal breathing is short and shallow, notice that, too, without judgment. If your breathing changes or stays the same, notice that. Don't try to change or fix anything. Don't think about "how things should be." Instead, accept things for what they are and just observe them without trying to control them.

For now, we are still observing your natural breathing pattern.

Sooner or later, you will lose your focus. That is perfectly normal, so don't criticize or judge yourself. We all get distracted, and focusing requires some practice.

Distractions always come from one of these sources: your thoughts, sensations, or feelings. When a distraction occurs, just notice it and let it go. Then, gently bring your focus back to your breath. Try to do it for a moment, until the next distraction. When you're distracted again, notice, and let it go. No need to push it away. Don't fight it, don't suppress it. Just let it float by.

Whenever your mind begins to wander, notice that too. Bring your attention back to your nose and the sensations in it as you breathe in and out.

It's also expected to feel the urge to name a distraction. For instance, you may mentally say to yourself, "The alarm is ringing in the next apartment", "kids are making noise outside", "there is traffic", "the dog's barking," or name whatever is distracting you.

Try to name just one thing instead, more general and more in connection with what's happening inside you—you can see "distraction" or "wandering", for instance. Always bring your attention back to your breathing. Try this for a moment, with the next distraction or when your mind wanders again.

Now, the next time you lose your focus, try not to name things at all—even mentally. Just notice that you have lost your focus and bring it back. Try doing this with the next distraction.

Most likely, depressed thoughts and feelings will intrude. These are the ones you are trying to escape from. The trick is to always bring your attention back to your breathing instead of following those thoughts.

Just breathe in your natural way. When a negative thought arises, just notice it and let it pass by. this will get easier each time because you already know how to let thoughts go by gently bringing your focus back to your nose and your breathing.

So try this for a moment. Notice the negative thought occurring. Let it float by you, easily, without your trying to push it away.

When you feel depressed, your mind is often stuck in the past, ruminating about some things from the past that have affected your life. Being in the present, and being consciously aware, makes you balanced. You are the most present when focusing on your breath and the sensations in your body. This focus makes you fully grounded in the present.

Try to be consciously present and aware of each moment of your next few breaths. Feel the air entering your nostrils. Feel its coolness. Feel it as it goes down your airways to your lungs and belly. Notice all the movements connected with your breath. Feel all the sensation it provokes in your body. Follow its way back, and feel the warmth of the air leaving your nostrils.

Doing this, be intentionally present and completely aware of every moment of your next few breaths.

Don't be surprised when negative emotions occur and distract you. These emotions go hand in hand with depressive thoughts. You'll probably feel emotions of sadness, emptiness, anxiety, resentment, bitterness, anger, or rage.

Emotions are nothing but a combination of your thoughts and your physical sensations. Acknowledge that fact, and mentally divide a negative emotion into those two parts. Notice the thought in your mind and feel the sensation it provokes in your body. You might feel the sensation as tension in your head or neck, weight on your chest, or fatigue, monotony, or an ache in various body parts. Allow yourself to experience what you feel. You don't need to change it, solve it, or take any action about it.

The second part is to see the thoughts in your mind. Acknowledge the connection between your thoughts and your physical sensations. Your thoughts provoke bodily sensations, and you experience those two together as an emotion.

Make a conscious choice to place your attention on a sensation in your body, not the thought. Rest your attention on the sensation. Notice if its intensity changes or stays the same. The sensation might even disappear under your focused attention.

Now, leave the emotion and the sensation in your body, and gently bring your attention back to your breathing and the way it feels in your nose. Breathe in, and feel the cool air entering your nose. Breathe out, and focus on the warmth of the air that's leaving your nose.

If you choose to follow your distressing thoughts, it will strengthen your connected negative sensations. But if you choose to pay undivided attention to your negative sensations, your depressing and distressing thoughts diminish. These sensations need your negative thoughts and their stories to feed themselves. So if you focus only on your physical sensations, negative emotions starve and fade away, bringing you relief.

Notice that focusing on your breathing and physical sensation grounds you in the present and brings you relief better than anything else.

Now, visualize that you are at a train station. People are rushing in all directions. There is hustle and bustle all around you. You are standing still on your platform, waiting for your train. The world around you seems dull and grey—colorless people wearing gray suits, dirty streets around the station, a gray station, and ugly trains. You are wearing a plain, gray robe with no defined shape. You are also carrying a heavy bag made of dark leather. It's so heavy that your arms are sore. But you can't put it down. You have to carry it wherever you go.

Thoughts may come and go in their rhythm while you observe the world around you. Don't worry, all the mental chatter will pass. Just let the thoughts be, and be gentle with yourself. Both people and your thoughts are passing by you in their busy manner, but you remain completely calm. You know you will be leaving this hectic environment in a moment, as soon as your train arrives.

Think of this moment as an escape that will help you think clearly again. The train will take you to a far destination, where you will feel peaceful and calm. You know you'll come back to this station as a different person. You are ready to begin the journey.

Your train arrives, and you are stepping aboard. Give yourself permission to devote this time to yourself, spend some time alone, and relax. You know you'll gain a new perspective, and you also know that this has to be done. So don't feel guilty.

You find your carriage. It's empty, and you are the only passenger here. Take a seat and finally put your heavy bag down. It's such a relief to finally put it down! Your muscles automatically relax. A sense of tranquility fills your mind and body.

Voices from the station start to fade away. You are looking through a window. It's the same dull and grey world out there, but you can observe it from a distance now. You are leaving it behind now, and it's natural to feel sadness, regret, or relief, knowing that you are leaving everything that was holding you back.

Take this your time to rest and relax. Allow yourself to see your needs and desires. Your sadness is trying to tell you something. Perhaps it's trying to show you that you have neglected your needs and needs of your soul. So your body suffers and processes unpleasant feelings to gain your attention. You have enough time now to relax the whole body.

You've created a distance now, and you can see your life from another perspective. From your window, the world outside looks different now. The sky looks bluer and clearer, and the grass and trees are greener.

The farther you get from the train station, the easier you feel. Your feel calm and positive. Your arms and hands are resting from carrying your heavy bag. Your muscles are relaxed in a comfortable seat. Your breathing is deep and slow. Your stomach is quiet and steady. Your legs and feet are comfortable and relaxed. Your mind slows down to a pleasant speed. You feel free to just be yourself, in balance, and let everything just be as it is.

As the train reaches your destination, it stops. You pick up your heavy, black bag and step off the train. You have just a few more streets to walk to your special place.

The bag is too heavy, but you know you won't have to carry it for much longer. You feel stronger now, as well as determined and enthusiastic.

You come to a stop in front of a large gate. You open it. You are in your private garden.

It's been a long time since you were here last time. The garden looks neglected. No one was taking care of it while you were occupied with your sadness and pain.

You step on the path that leads through the garden. There are no flowers or grass. Instead, there are weeds.

You go to an old tree at the back of the garden. There's a spade leaning against a tree. You take it and starting to dig. You dig a hole in the shade of the tree. Once you're done digging, you open the bag, curious to find out what was the heavy load you were carrying around.

To your surprise, the bag is full of your worries, fears, sadness, anger, and regrets. You can see them all as large, heavy stones. It's time to bury them now.

Now, take the rocks, one by one, and drop them into the hole you've dug. Name your stones by your unpleasant feelings and mentally say to each of them while dropping it into the hole, "I'm letting you go."

Let go of sadness.

Let go of regrets.

Let go of anger.
Let go of self-doubt.
Let go of resentment.
Let go of bitterness.
Let go of monotony.
Let go of hatred.
Let go of jealousy.
Let go of misery.
Let go of helplessness.
Let go of hopelessness.
Let go of fears.
Let go of the pain.
Let go of suffering.
Let go of everything that makes you feel bad.

Do this as long as you need to bury all the stones from your bag. In the end, bury the bag too. Recover the hole with dirt, and feel the relief.

Now, go back to an old bench in the middle of the garden. Take a seat on the bench and enjoy the feeling of ease and freedom. Feel the lightness. Notice the sun shining through the trees. Look around.

Nurturing this garden needs just a little energy to fix everything and bring back its old glow. Taking care of this place is your priority now. You know you'll enjoy every moment of it and the results of tending to it.

Rest deeply in your garden, imaging its final look once you've taken care of everything. Inhale the sunlight. Exhale peace. Look at the colorful flowers. Smell the roses. Feel your enthusiasm. Realize that your journey brought you here to remind you of who you really are. Your old self is back now.

Smile at who you really are. Enjoy watching the dance of light and shadows in your garden, and mentally say to yourself:

*I am free.*
*I am relaxed.*
*I am peaceful.*
*I am grateful.*
*I am light.*
*I am happy.*
*I am energetic.*
*I am full of love.*
*I am calm.*
*I am safe.*
*I am powerful.*
*I am joyful.*
*Life is good.*
*Life is colorful.*
*Life is magnificent.*
*I love myself.*
*I know my value.*
*I appreciate myself.*
*I accept myself.*
*I love life.*

*I am free.*
*I am relaxed.*
*I am peaceful.*
*I am grateful.*
*I am light.*
*I am happy.*
*I am energetic.*
*I am full of love.*
*I am calm.*
*I am safe.*
*I am powerful.*
*I am joyful.*
*Life is good.*
*Life is colorful.*
*Life is magnificent.*
*I love myself.*
*I know my value.*
*I appreciate myself.*
*I accept myself.*
*I love life.*

Breathe deeply, and smile to yourself with every exhale.

Enjoy being in this relaxed state for a while, feeling the warm sunlight on your skin. You can take this feeling with you wherever you go.

When you come back from this trip to your usual life, you will have a completely different perspective. Your private garden will always be there for you. You can come back to it whenever you wish.

When you feel ready, gently open your eyes and go on with your usual daily activities. Or, you can drift off to sleep and have a deep rest.

# Guided Meditation for Overcoming Insomnia

Good evening. Welcome to this guided meditation that will help you overcome insomnia.
If you have problems with falling asleep or staying asleep during the night, this meditation is for you. You can use it whether you frequently have trouble sleeping, or just from time to time.
It's not pleasant at all to lie sleeplessly in your bed and feel exhausted the next day, unable to give a quality rest to your body and mind.
Use this meditation before sleep as part of your evening routine.
Prepare yourself for bed in your usual way. Lie down on your bed and find the most comfortable position. The temperature should also be pleasant—not too warm, not too cold. You can lie on your back or on your side—whatever position best helps you relax.
I invite you to listen to my voice. Let my voice guide you, help you relax, and take you to a calm, calm state from which you can easily fall asleep.
My words in this meditation will speak to your both conscious and subconscious mind. That way, I will help you easily fall asleep and stay asleep for the whole night.
Finally, you'll have a restful sleep that will recharge you. The sleep you'll enjoy will be the first time in a long time that you won't wake up during the night. You'll finally feel rested and refreshed in the morning. However, this might not happen the first few times you do this meditation. But what will undoubtedly happen is that you will relax more and feel less tensed.
A good night's sleep is a habit. To build a habit of easily falling asleep and staying asleep throughout the night, you will need time and practice. But once you've established this habit, it will pay off in levels of energy and life satisfaction. So it's worth a try.
I recommend that you be patient and consistent in using this meditation every night before sleep. It will undoubtedly lead to forming better sleep habits, and eventually overcoming insomnia. The first time you fall asleep and stay asleep until the morning, waking up renewed and refreshed, you'll realize that all your efforts have paid off and this was the best thing you could do for yourself.
We often have a hard time trying to relax and fall asleep because our minds refuse to stop thinking. When our body tries to calm down to sleep, our brain seems to find it the best time to go into overdrive. If you are one of many people who overthink, especially when it's time for sleep, you can't stop thinking. It would be best to write all your thoughts down. That way, you'll put these thoughts aside for later, without any worry that you might forget something important. You'll also free up space in your mind, allowing it to calm down.
So, pause this meditation and transfer all your pressing thoughts from your mind to a piece of paper. Your concerns and actions can wait. Now, it is time for rest.
I now invite you to put your attention on my voice and ground yourself in this very moment. Feel the comfort and the warmth of your bed. Feel the ease, because it is a time when you don't need to do anything. This is time only for you and your reenergizing.
You don't have to do a thing. Just listen to my voice without any expectation, especially an expectation of falling asleep. Even if you stay awake all night long, this meditation will still bring you relaxation and rest. So don't put any pressure on yourself. All you need to do is lie in your bed, listen to my words, and relax. If sleep comes, great. If not, no big deal. You will still get rest.
Take a deep breath in, to the count of four. Hold the breath to the count of three. Breathe out as slowly as you can, counting to six.

Repeat this sequence a few more times. Take a deep breath in, to the count of four. Hold the breath to the count of three. Breathe out as slowly as you can, counting to six.

Do it once again Inhale—one, two, three, four. Hold it—one, two, three. Exhale—one, two, three, four, five, six.

And one more time, breathe in deeply, counting to four. Hold the breath the count of three. Then breathe out, counting to six.

If you can't reach these numbers, that's okay. Don't force yourself—just do what you can.

Then, allow your breathing to fall back into its usual rhythm.

With each breath out, allow your body to relax a bit more and sink deeper into the surface beneath you. Now, watch your thoughts come and go. They come and go all the time. Your busy mind is used to producing them all the time. But you don't have to follow each and every one of them.

This insight is a precious one—you are not your thoughts. Even more so, you can always choose which of your thoughts you want to think about. Your thoughts are just products of your mind, and you are the one who decides which ones to think about.

So if you're going to rest your busy mind and fall asleep, let your thoughts float by like little clouds or soap bubbles. Since you can't forbid your mind to do its job and create thoughts, the only thing you can do is to remove your focus from your thoughts. Focus on something else, and unwanted thoughts will lose their power and diminish. Eventually, your mind will slow down and stop creating them. That's why mindful focus on your breathing, physical sensations, and environment can go a long way to relax and calm a busy mind.

Now, bring your awareness to your body and its sensations. This is always the first step towards mindful presence.

Notice how your body feels. Acknowledge its posture, and feel the temperature of your body and the space around it. Feel the support of the surface beneath you and the comfort of your mattress. Feel the weight of your body and the weights of bed covers on top of you. Feel your heartbeat and the rhythm of your blood flow. Focus on your breathing and listen to its sounds.

Place your attention on your nose. Feel the air entering your nostrils and going down to fill your lungs. Note how you fill your stomach with the air and allow your stomach to inflate like a balloon. Then, follow the way of the breath back, noticing how it leaves your stomach, your lungs, and finally, your nostrils. Notice the coolness of the air you are inhaling, and the warmth of it when you exhale it after it went through your body.

Continue to focus only on your breathing and movement, along with the sensations it provokes in your body. This process is the easiest and quickest way to ground yourself and relax.

How do your feet feel? How do your legs feel? Notice sensations in each part of the body. How do your glutes and pelvic area feel? What do you feel in your stomach? How does your back feel? Notice all the sensations in your fingers, hands, and arms. Acknowledge how your shoulders and neck feel. Then, bring your awareness to sensations in your head and face.

If there is any tension in your body, acknowledge it. Allow all the tension to rise from the deep or hidden corners of your body, coming up to the surface. When you feel that all the tension is collecting on your skin, let it go.

Take a deep breath, and with your exhale, let go of tension.

Repeat this process a few times until you feel your body is completely relaxed, free from any tension.

Do another quick scan of the whole body, part by part, checking if all the parts are relaxed.

If you find any tension, simply let it go with breathing out.

There are so many things you can place your focus on right now. Even the busiest mind calms when you are mindful and truly present.

Sooner or later, your focus will drift off from your breathing and physical sensations. Gently bring your focus back. Concentrating on the feelings in your body and on your breathing is the simplest, yet most powerful way to stay present, grounded, calm, and relaxed.

Thoughts will eventually appear in your mind. Don't stress about that happening. Notice your thoughts, and let them go. Do this as many times as needed, always bringing your focus back to your breath and your body. Notice the air entering your nose, and stay with the breath throughout the body, moment by moment. This is a natural way to calm yourself and, after some time, drift off to sleep.

So breathe in, breathe out, and, with a smile, greet the wonderful feeling of relaxation and letting go. This is time only for you. This is time to recharge and gain fresh energy.

Stretch your body and feel how comfortable it is to lie in your bed, having nothing else to do. The night is meant for having rest from everyone and everything, including our thoughts. So with every breath, dive deeper into the sense of comfort and relaxation.

Now, visualize that you are on a canoe on calm, clear water. The canoe is floating on the water, cradling you gently. Listen to the lapping sounds of the water. Your eyes are closed, and the sun is shining tenderly on your skin. Your boat is incredibly comfortable, as soft as a cloud, yet strong enough to support you. You are safe and calm.

Feel the joy and the ease of this moment. It's beautiful. Breathe in, breathe out, and smile to yourself.

The canoe is large enough for your whole body to lie down comfortably. It's time for you to relax the whole body, part by part, by scanning it with your mindful attention, healing light, and your inner smile. Begin by relaxing your toes and feet. Allow them to gently open to the ceiling. Relax all the muscles of your legs. Relax your lower and upper legs. Relax your knees. Relax your hips and pelvic area. Relax your glutes, and notice how now the whole lower part of your body is relaxed. Allow your fingers to relax, and open your palms to the ceiling. Relax your wrists, and all of your hands and arms.

Place your inner smile into your belly. Feel the calmness and peace in your stomach. Allow it to move easily in the rhythm of your breathing. Notice how relaxed it is. Relax your chest, and feel it floating.

Now, relax your back from the lowest point up to your neck. Relax your vertebrae, one by one, and feel each muscle loosening and relaxing. Your back becomes soft, as during a massage. Breathe in and breathe out, visualizing that you are exhaling through your spine everything you want to let go.

Our shoulders are the most crucial area in relaxation. They are where we hold and carry most of the weight, such as our worries, fears, and uncomfortable feelings. Most of us go through life not noticing that our shoulders are tensed and tight. So relax your shoulders now. Let go of all the weight, and let your shoulders drop from your ears.

Relax your neck, allowing it to loosen and soften, leaving your head cradled by the soft pillow. Open up your throat and allow all the muscles in there to relax.

The muscles of the head are often tensed and overwhelmed. Let all these muscles relax. Relax your scalp and your forehead. Relax your eyebrows, and all the tiny muscles around your eyes. Allow your eyes to rest into the head. They work hard all day long, so it's time for them to finally have a proper rest.

Relax your cheeks and your lips. Release your jaw and allow the base of your tongue to relax. Relax your ears.

Intentionally release any other tension you might be still feeling in your head and face.

Once again, do another quick scan of the whole body to check that it is completely relaxed.

Your feet—relaxed. Your legs, knees, upper legs—relaxed. Your hips and pelvis—relaxed. Your glutes—relaxed. Your hands—relaxed. Your arms, elbows, and upper arms—relaxed. Your belly—relaxed. Your chest—relaxed. Your back, from the bottom to the top—relaxed. Your shoulders and neck—relaxed. The top of your bead and the back of your head—relaxed. Your face—relaxed. Your eye muscles, your nose, your cheeks, your mouth, your jaw—all relaxed.

Now, when all the parts of your body are relaxed, it's time to pay attention to your skin and allow it to relax too. Your skin works all the time, protecting your body from the outside world. It also needs rest and reenergizing.

Now, visualize the other organs in your body. Take a moment to appreciate everything they do for you all the time. Smile at them with your inner smile, send them love and light, and allow them to relax. Imagine your body on the inside. Imagine your organs working for you all the time. Mentally send them love, and let them relax.

Acknowledge that your emotional parts also need rest. Emotions are turned on all the time, but you don't need them to be on right now. Give your emotions permission to let go. Forgive everything there is to be forgiven. Let go of all negative feelings. The only thing you need now is inner peace and tranquility. Don't hold any anger, resentment, nor sadness. Let go of everything that doesn't serve you.

If any thoughts occur, and they certainly will, let them pass you by. You don't need any of them right now. It is not time to think about or solve problems, be productive, or achieve anything. It is time to rest your mind. Let your mind rest and recharge now so you can be productive when the time for that comes.

Now, visualize you are in a dark, empty room. The only thing you can see is a clock on the wall. The clock hands are moving at the speed of your thoughts. The only thing you should do is count the movements of the clock hands.

You find counting the hands' movements harder and harder, because they move slower and slower. You are becoming more and more sleepy. You notice the hands' movements become slower and slower until they are barely moving at all.

Your mind is calm and clear now. You are just a step away from drifting off to sleep.

Observe your body becoming heavier and sleepier. You are in a state of deep relaxation now. Watch your slow and deep breathing, your calm mind, and your relaxed body. There's no need to change anything. There's only calm, mindful observation and acceptance. You feel the warmth, coziness, peace, and deep calmness. Everything's calm, peaceful, and easy. Everything you don't need fades away into the blurry background. Inhale. Exhale.

This is how it feels to be relaxed on a deep level.

You are carefree. All is well. Breathe in, breathe out.

Let go of all your concerns, fears, and worries. Everything will be just fine. Everything happens when the time is perfect. Leave everything to higher intelligence, and trust all will be well.

Enjoy the serenity and carefreeness of giving up control, and allow a dream to come.

This is a moment of perfect balance and harmony.

Notice your deep, calm breathing. Feel the comfort and ease of becoming one with the moment, releasing any effort. Your body and mind are enjoying these moments of absolute rest.

You are now in a forest, high in the mountains. The sun is shining through the trees. You've been hiking in the forest all day long. You feel pretty tired now, but your house is still quite far away. So you have to walk about an hour more until you get there. You know that a fire in the fireplace, a cozy blanket, and a warm, comfortable bed are waiting for you.

You're stepping down a steep, narrow path. You feel so tired that you start to count your steps to move your attention from your sore feet. You are walking and breathing in the fresh mountain air, counting your breaths one by one. Breathe in, breathe out—one. Breathe in, breathe out—two. Breathe in, breathe out—three. Breathe in, breathe out—four. Breathe in, breathe out—five.

Your feet are tired. Your legs are sleepy. Your back needs rest. Your mind is sluggish. Your eyes are struggling to stay open. Your hands are limp. You are yawning, wishing only one thing—to get to your house soon and sink into bed.

You're going down the steep path. You know you have to get home before the day ends. You can hear birds and insects in the grass, your steps down the path, and the sound of your breathing.

You are still breathing deeply, counting each inhale and exhale. The night is about to come. The forest is preparing for sleep. It becomes harder and harder to walk and count as you become more and more sleepy. You wish to lie under the tree and just let yourself fall asleep.

You are yawning and can barely walk. Fortunately, just a few more steps, and you'll get to the small house where you can finally sleep. The moon and stars appear in the sky.

You finally reach your destination. You open the wooden door. Your legs are heavy, and you can barely move. A warm fire is crackling in the fireplace.

You lie down on your cozy bed, placing your head onto a soft, fluffy pillow, wrapping yourself in a warm blanket.

You can feel your legs are already sleeping. Your stomach is sleeping. Your back is sleeping. Your head is sleeping. Your face is sleeping. Your whole body is sleeping. It's now time to allow your mind to fall asleep too.

Mentally repeat those statements:

*I am calm.*
*I am peaceful.*
*I am tranquil.*
*I am free.*
*I am worth everything life has to give me.*
*I am full of love.*
*I am healing.*
*I am recharging.*
*I am reenergizing.*
*I am resting.*
*I am divinely supported and guided.*
*I am safe.*
*I am secure.*
*I feel good.*
*I feel comfortable.*
*I feel light.*
*I feel serene.*
*Everything's all right.*
*I'm free to rest now.*

While you fall asleep, acknowledge that all is well. You'll have a good, quality rest tonight. You'll fall asleep now, and stay asleep throughout the whole night. In the morning, you'll wake up refreshed and renewed.

Feel the serenity. Feel the calmness. Feel the tranquility and deep peace. Allow yourself to sink into a deeper sleep, knowing everything is fine. You are calm. You are safe. You are worthy. You deserve good rest.

Step into the sleeping state, where all the problems of the day are solved.

Good night, and have a nice sleep.

# 10 Guided Meditations For Anxiety, Depression & Deep Sleep:

## Positive Affirmations & Meditation Scripts For Relaxation, Self-Healing, Overthinking, Stress-Relief & Rapid Weight Loss

Healing Mindfulness & Hypnosis Buddy

© **Copyright 2021 - All rights reserved.**

The content contained within this book may not be reproduced, duplicated or transmitted without direct written permission from the author or the publisher.
Under no circumstances will any blame or legal responsibility be held against the publisher, or author, for any damages, reparation, or monetary loss due to the information contained within this book; either directly or indirectly.

Legal Notice:
This book is copyright protected. This book is only for personal use. You cannot amend, distribute, sell, use, quote or paraphrase any part, or the content within this book, without the consent of the author or publisher.

Disclaimer Notice:
Please note the information contained within this document is for educational and entertainment purposes only. All effort has been executed to present accurate, up to date, and reliable, complete information. No warranties of any kind are declared or implied. Readers acknowledge that the author is not engaging in the rendering of legal, financial, medical or professional advice.

# Table Of Content

Guided meditation for relaxation ................................................................................................ 64

Guided Meditation For Stress Relief ........................................................................................... 69

Guided Meditation For Self-healing ............................................................................................ 76

Affirmations for self-healing ....................................................................................................... 81

Meditation for Rapid Weight Loss ............................................................................................... 84

Guided Meditation For Overthinking .......................................................................................... 91

Guided Meditation To Stop Overthinking 2 ................................................................................ 94

Guided Mindfulness Meditation for Overcoming Anxiety ......................................................... 96

Affirmations for overcoming anxiety ........................................................................................ 100

Guided Meditation For Overcoming Depression ...................................................................... 104

Guided Meditation For Overcoming Insomnia ......................................................................... 111

Guided Meditation For Self-healing While Sleeping ................................................................ 116

Affirmations for reprogramming your subconsciousness while sleeping ................................. 120

# Guided meditation for relaxation

50 minutes

Welcome to the meditation for deep relaxation.
This meditation will help you release all the tension from your body and mind and relax on a deeper level.
Relaxation is vital for our physical and mental health.
When we relax, everything that we want is coming our way.
Our mind gets enough time to rest and repair itself, and our body releases all the tension we are carrying around, getting an opportunity to fix all the tiny problems that might occur.
People who find ways to relax and practice it regularly are healthier, happier, live more fulfilled lives, and have a longer lifespan.
However, most of us overlook relaxing activities, always in a rush to achieve more and more. We go through our lives with tensed shoulders, frantic minds, and chaotic thoughts. We often forget to stop to smell roses and enjoy the journey.
It's time to change this once for good. Meditation is a proven way to relax completely, on a deeper level, and achieve a state of inner peace and complete calmness.
You won't need long before you fall in love with this practice. It's something like lying in the sun on hot sand, listening to waves, being massaged and gently lulled at the same time.
So, you don't have to do a thing. Just listen to my voice and follow my guidance. I will gently guide you through the process of deep relaxation. From there, you can easily drift off to sleep or move on with your usual activities. We'll relax the whole body, part by part. Then we'll go to your mind and emotions.

So, let's begin.
Lie down and make yourself comfortable. Find the most convenient position and posture. Make sure that all the parts of your body can rest and relax on the surface. Use a blanket if needed to make yourself pleasantly warm. Nothing should be bothering you, not even clothes nor other ordinary inconveniences.
Gently close your eyes and bring your attention to the center of your body.
Take a nice, deep breath. Exhale slowly.
This is the time just for you. It's time to do what's needed for your highest good. There's nothing else you should be doing right now. Bring all of your attention to this moment. This moment is the only reality that exists for you.
Take another deep breath through the nose. Engage your belly, allowing it to move in the rhythm of your breathing. Breathe out through your mouth, slowly, and notice how your whole body relaxes on the exhale. Breath-outs longer than breath-ins help you calm and relax. When you do so, your mind is getting signals that everything's perfectly fine and it can relax. This technique is powerful to apply whenever you feel tensed or anxious throughout the day, not only during a meditation session.
Breathe in slowly. Breathe out even slower.

Once again, take a long breath in. Then breathe out slowly.

Just observe natural breathing rhythm without trying to control it nor change it. Just watch and enjoy the experience of breathing in and out.

It's ridiculous how often we can't do something without someone's permission. We are even waiting for someone's permission to relax. So, permit yourself to do it. It's vital and precious for you and everyone around you. You deserve these moments of joy and deep relaxation. Give up the urge to control everything. Let it go.

Bring your attention back to your breathing.

Observe the way the air goes through your body. Watch it and feel it entering your nostrils, going down to your lungs and down to your belly. Feel your abdominals expanding, like a balloon on the inhale and contracting it on the exhale.

This meditation is here to help you relax completely, so please, let go of any other expectations you might have. Don't expect any insights to come or some particular change to take place during the meditation session. Doing this regularly will bring you the wanted changes. But, for now, the best you can do is being consciously present, focused on this very moment. This is not time to think nor take action. The most productive thing you can do now is to relax.

If you notice your mind is not calm as you might be wanting, don't worry. Having internal chatters and random thoughts is totally normal. Notice you have some internal talk going on. Notice random thoughts arising in your mind. Just notice their existence and let them go. Watch them passing by without engaging. If something popped up in your mind, it doesn't mean you have to give it your attention. Consciously choose to stay aside of it, observing, not engaging. Slowly, they'll fade away, slipping into the background rumor.

Don't be concerned in any way. This is how your mind works - it is meant to produce thoughts all the time. You can't just switch it off. In the end, you are meditating, not dead. It will take some time and practice for your mind to learn to relax and have some time free from duty, and you'll be surprised how calm it can be. But, for now, let it do what it wants and control what you can - your attention. And at this moment, your attention is on relaxing your body.

Bring your attention to your breath. Breathe in to the count of four. One, two, three, four.
Hold it to the count of three. One, two, three.
Breathe out, counting to seven. One, two, three, four, five, six, seven.
Repeat - breathe in to the count of four.
One, two, three, four.
Hold your breath to the count of three - one, two, three.
Exhale, to the count of seven - one, two, three, four, five, six, seven.
Do it once again.
Inhale, counting to four.
Hold, counting to three.
Exhale, to the count of seven.
Now, let your breathing settle in its natural pattern.

Now, bring your attention to sensations in your body. Notice how it feels. Try to locate parts where you feel some tension. Perhaps you can feel it in your shoulders, in your jaw, or neck. Maybe your back is tensed. Just notice where you are holding tension in your body and make a mental note for later.

Your body does so much for you - it carries your spirit around, it serves you in so many ways, from representing you to the world to feel the world with senses. Mentally thank it for being there for you. Your body deserves those moments of deep relaxation.
Let's begin with relaxing it, part by part.

Put all the attention to your feet. Feel your toes, your heels, and the whole feet. Breathe in and tense your feet a bit. Feel aliveness in them. Breathe out, releasing all the tension from your feet. Relax your toes, your heels, your ankles.
Bring your attention up to your calf muscles. Breathe in and feel them. Breathe out, and relax your calf muscles. Relax your knees, your whole legs. Squeeze your thigh muscles, feel the tension in them. Exhale and lose them up. Relax your thighs and your hips. Allow them to open up. Relax your pelvic area, and feel the glutes on the surface beneath you. Relax your glutes.
Take a nice, deep breath again, and exhaling, relax your lower body again. Feel complete relaxation in your legs, hips, glutes. The lower half of your body is already enjoying complete relaxation now.

Bring your focus to your hands now. Feel aliveness in your fingers and palms, opened up to the ceiling. Feel the tingling in your fingertips. With every breath out, relax your fingers, one by one. Breathe in, breathe out, relaxing your left and your right pinky finger. Breathe in, and breathe out, relaxing your ring fingers. Take a breath, then breathe out, relaxing both your middle fingers. Inhale, then exhaling, relax your index fingers, left and right. Take one more breath. Breathe out slowly, allowing your thumbs to relax.
 Bring attention to your palms. They do so much work, yet, they never had relaxation time. Breathe in, breathe out, and consciously relax your palms.

Inhale, and tighten your lower arms and elbows. Feel the tightness in your upper arms. Hold the breath for a moment. Three, two, one, and release tension. Feel all the muscles in your arms loosen and relax.
With the next breath in, tense up your shoulders and lift them up so they can almost touch your ears. Hold the breath - three, two, one. Breathe out and relax your shoulders. Let them loosen and drop down.
Our shoulders are often the place where we hold most of our burden - all the stress, worries, tension. Let it all drop from your shoulders now.  Take a breath, and with the exhale, let all the weight fall from you.
Now, contract your abdominal muscles as tightly as you can. Pull them to your spine to feel the tension. Hold for a moment—three, two, one, and release. Relax your stomach and allow it to turn into its natural rhythm of moving with your breath.
With the next breath, fill your lungs and tense up your chest. Hold to the count of three, two, one. Breathe out, relaxing your chest. Feel your ribcage is floating, relaxed.
Stretch the muscles of your back. Feel the tension in the back and your spine. Hold the breath - three, two, one. Breathe out, relaxing all the back muscles, one by one.
Repeat this for the lower back, for the middle, and the upper back.

Inhale, tense the muscles of your lower back. Hold - three, two, one. Breathe out, and relax your lower back muscles.

With the nest breath, feel the tension in the middle part of your back. With the exhale, relax those muscles. Tighten your upper back muscles. Hold for three, two, one. And relax.

Stretch your neck and tense it while breathing in. Hold the breath - three, two, one. Release the breath and relax your neck.

With the next breath, feel the tension in your scalp. Stay with the sensation for three, two, one. Breathe out and allow your scalp to relax.

Feel the intense tension in your forehead. This part is often too tensed due to overthinking. Tense it even more by raising your eyebrows. Hold it tensed for three, two, one. Then release. Breathe out and relax your forehead, allowing all the tension to drift away.

Breathe in and squeeze your eyes, tensing all the tiny eye muscles. Hold it tight for three, two, one. Then, breathe out and relax your eyes. Loosen all the muscles around them and allow your eyes to sink into the head.

Clench your teeth and the jaw with the next breath. Hold it to three, two, one. Breathe out and release. Allow your jaw to drop so your teeth aren't touching. Relax your lips and release tension in your tongue base.

Now your whole body is relaxed. Scan it mentally once again. If you feel tension anywhere, make a conscious choice, and put the intentional effort into relaxing that area.

Now, visualize you are on a beautiful beach.

You are lying on the warm sand. It's soft and glittering, and it shapes to support your body perfectly. It feels like a massage.

You can feel smooth sand gently massaging the back of your legs, your glutes, your back, your neck, and the back of your head.

The temperature of the air is pleasantly warm. You can feel the fresh, salty smell of the ocean in your nostrils. Breathe in and fill your lungs. Breathing out, release any remaining tension into the golden sand beneath you. It's absorbing all the negativity, tension, and worries from your body. Everything you don't want anymore, you can give to the sand to take it down into the ground and the ocean.

You can hear the waves rolling in, curl over and dissolve into foam. Breathe deeply and enjoy this relaxing sound. Rest your hands on the warm sand, rest your back, and your head, supported by the surface. Focus on the sound. Breathe with your belly. There's nothing else you should be doing right now, nor anywhere else you should be now. You are in the right place, doing the right thing. Enjoy the sun rays on your skin and the touch of the sand beneath you.

Now, you can feel something more - like a gentle tickling on your feet. It stops for a moment. You can feel the same sensation in the next moment, but this time, it spreads to your ankles. You realize it's foam - the waves are reaching you. It disappears again, and in the next moment, you feel the water again; this time it's getting your legs to the knees.

You are enjoying the fresh touch of the water and have no intention to move. You know something wonderful is about to happen, and you also know that you are completely safe and sound.

Breathe in. Feel the touch of freshness on your thighs. Breathe out, and let the water take away any tension remaining. Breathe in.

Feel the foam reaching your hips and glutes. Breathe out and release everything you don't want anymore / any stress, worries, fear / allow it all goes with the water.

Take a breath in. Feel the foam on your belly and your lower back. AS the water flow back, breathe out, letting it take away any negativity from your abdominal area or your lower back.

Breathe in. Feel the water on your chest and your upper back. Breathe out everything you want it to take away.

As the wave reaches your shoulders and head, you can feel you are being lifted from the sand beneath you. Now you are floating on the water and being gently taken with the wave.

Your body is floating on the sparkling sea surface now.

This floating is so relaxing, and you know it's also healing.

Enjoy this unique experience of allowing and letting go of control. Feel you're light and easy, like being flying and supported at the same time. It feels like lying on a large, soft pillow. Enjoy the sensation of weightlessness. The sea surface is sparkling, still like glass.

Everything you don't want drains out from your body and disappears in a deep blue. All the old energy from your body is replaced with the new, fresh one. Feel free to dive into the water. All the thoughts and worries from your head flow out to the water. Your mind is clear and refreshed. Allow your internal organs to relax. Imagine them being bathed by healthy, salty, golden water. Relax your skin. Relax your emotions. Give them permission to leave you.

You are completely relaxed on the deepest level now.

Enjoy his lightness and gentle floating for as long as you like. From here, you can drift off to sleep, lulled by the soft swing and sound of the sea. Or, visualize you are opening your eyes and slowly swimming to the shore. You feel fresh and renewed, energized, and ready for the day.

# Guided Meditation For Stress Relief

60 min

Welcome to the meditation for stress relief.
We all live stressful lives nowadays. We have way too long to-do lists, yet only 24 hours in a day; stressful jobs, all those terrible things from news and all over the internet... we all live in uncertain times, and it's not surprising we go through our lives with our shoulders tensed, with clenched jaws and fists, always ready to fight or flight. If this sounds familiar, don't worry, you are in the right place.

Though small doses of stress won't hurt you but help you stay alert and productive, living with chronic stress is exhausting and dangerous. Not only that it drains your energy, but it will damage your health and negatively impact all the life fields.

Meditation is the most powerful way to release stress, vent out and relax completely. If you do it regularly, you won't hold toxic tension in your body so that it won't do you any harm. So, do yourself a favor and intentionally take some time in a day to relax and decompress.

Listen to my voice and follow my guidance. I'll help you calm and ease the stress. You don't have to think about anything, just follow simple instructions and focus on the inside.
By practicing this meditation, you'll learn some efficient techniques for stress relief. You can use them whenever you feel levels of stress become disturbing. Whenever you feel stressed, or you had a stressful situation, or if you know something stressful is ahead of you, use those techniques to relax and stay calm.

Pick a time in the day when you know you can be alone and not disturbed for a while. Choose a place where you can have some peace. Turn off all distractions - such as notifications, rings, and so. The world won't stop spinning around if you take some time just for yourself to let go of stress and find your inner balance.

Our natural state is ease, peace, and joy. Allowing ourselves to be stressed all the time takes us further and further from our true nature and inner balance. There's nothing natural in being stressed. Have you ever heard of a stressed lion or a tensed bird in a wood? That's just something we have learned to live with. But our mind still needs some time to calm, relax, process. Our body needs to rest from tension, so it can energize and heal itself.

Stress affects the body as mind. That's why we'll combat it on all levels. Due to high levels of stress, our breathing becomes short and shallow. That's why our first step is to deepen your breathing and slow it down. Then, you'll relax the whole body, part by part. And, finally, you'll calm your mind, free it from stressful thoughts and let it relax.

Make yourself comfortable and find an effortless position, sit or lie down and straighten your back.

Bring your attention to this moment. Be there, aware of the moment and your body, the space around you. Try not to judge nor to expect anything to happen. You'll notice numerous thoughts are popping up in your mind. And it's normal, so don't stress about it. That's the way the human brain works. It's his job to produce thoughts. But you can simply let them go. Just observe them without engaging. Since you already feel stressed, most of your thoughts create stress. But, if you decide to let them go, that's the end; they won't work anymore. So, don't engage; just let them float by. You are focused only on relaxation now.

Pick a random point in your sight, above your head. Focus on that point. Watch it very carefully until you feel your eyes are getting tired. Then gently close them. It feels so good to close your eyes.
Now, acknowledge your breathing. Observe it as thoroughly as you can. Feel the freshness of the air entering your nose. Try to follow its way down through your airways to your lungs. Feel the air expanding your belly, then leaving it, allowing it to fall. Scan with your attention the way of the air back and feel it leaves your nostrils, warmer than it was at first. Acknowledge all the movements and sensations in the body that breath provokes. It's so essential yet magnificent activity, one of many that our bodies perform for us. And it works without you even thinking where your next breath will come from.

Now, let's deepen your breath. Take a breath, counting to four. One, two, three, four.
Hold the breath to the count of three. One, two, three.
Breathe out to the count of six. One, two, three, four, five, six.
Repeat it once again.
Inhale - one, two, three, four.
Hold - one, two, three.
Exhale - one, two, three, four, five, six.
Imagine all the stress from your body is assembling in a giant bubble. Slowly breathe out and visualize you are blowing it away. See the bubble flies up and up into the sky, pops, and all of your stress pulverizes.

Take a nice, deep breath, and visualize you are inhaling peace. Exhale tension.
Inhale tranquility. Breathe out slowly, telling yourself: relax.
Focus your undivided attention on your breathing. Breathe deeply and slowly. Enjoy this experience, maybe for the first time seeing your breathing as a wonderful action as it really is.

When you notice random thoughts popping up in your mind, don't stress yourself. Just let them pass by. Notice them appearing, then allow them to fly by, and gently bring your attention back to your breathing. Observe its rhythm and the physical sensations it provokes.

Conscious breathing will always call you back to mindful presence. It's the quickest and most natural way to relax and relieve stress. Use it whenever you feel the need to reduce tension. Your breath is the most precious gift that's given you to last as long as you live. It's the connection between your spiritual and physical existence, and it's always with you. Appreciate it for a moment. Mentally thank your breath for keeping you alive.

Although we are so used to live with it, stress is hazardous to our mind, body, and health overall. It affects all the organs and systems, every tiny cell in our body. It's such a heavy burden for our mind that it can't do what it's capable of.

The human body has an extraordinary power to repair and heal itself. However, stress makes it impossible. Living with chronic stress is the same as living with toxins that poison you from the inside. That's why regular relaxation is a must, like nurturing your body healthy food or brushing your teeth. It's not a luxury but a basic need.

You can't relax your mind without relaxing your body first. That's why we're going to relax the body as our first step. You'll tense up all the muscles, then allow them to relax completely. Repeat this with each part of the body until it's whole deeply relaxed.

Invite your attention to your toes. Breathe in, tensing up your feet. Count: three, two, one, holding your breath and your feet tensed. Then breathe out and release.

With the next breath, tense up your lower legs and knees. Hold it for a moment- three, two, one. Breathe out and relax.
Take another deep breath and tense your upper legs and hips as tight as you can. Hold your breath - three, two, one. And release the tightness with the breath out.

With the next breath in, squeeze your glutes. Hold it tight for a moment. Three, two, one. Breathe out, and allow the muscles to relax.

Inhale deeply and clench your fists. Hold it to the count of three - three, two, one. On the exhale, let your fingers and hands loosen. Relax your palms, and allow them to open against the ceiling. Loosen your wrists.

Take a deep breath, and tighten your lower arms and elbows. Hold the breath and tightness in your arms for a moment. Three, two, one. Release tension and notice all the muscles in your arms loosen and relax.

With the next inhale, tense up your shoulders and lift them up so they can almost touch your ears. Hold the breath - three, two, one. Breathe out and let your shoulders loosen and drop.

Our shoulders are where we hold most of the weight - all the stress, tension, worries. Let it all drop from your shoulders now. Now allow all the weight to fall from you.

Now, pull your navel to your spine, contract your abdominal muscles as tightly as you can. Hold the tension for a moment—three, two, one, and release. Relax your belly and let it fall into its natural movement in the rhythm of your breathing.

With the next breath, fill your lungs and tense up your chest. Hold to the count of three, two, one. Breathe out, relaxing the muscles of your chest. Feel your ribcage is floating.

Stretch your back and spine. Feel the tension in the back muscles. Hold the breath - three, two, one. Breathe out, loosening all the back muscles, one by one. Relax your back muscles and let them melt down like being massaged with your awareness. Start with the lower back, then relax the middle and the upper back muscles.

Feel the muscles of your neck tensing up while breathing in. Hold the breath - three, two, one. Slowly breathe out, allowing your neck to relax.

With the next breath, tense up in your scalp. Stay with the sensation for three, two, one. Breathe out and allow your scalp to relax.

Bring awareness to your forehead and feel the intense tension there. This part is often too tensed due to overthinking. Raise your eyebrows to tense it even more. Hold it for three, two, one. Breathe out and relax your forehead; let all the tension drift away.

With the next breath in, squeeze your eyes. Tense all the tiny eye muscles. Hold it tight for three, two, one. Then, breathe out and relax your eyes. Allow your eyes to sink into the head and loosen muscles around them.

With the next breath in, clench your teeth and the jaw. Hold it tensed while counting three, two, one. Breathe out and release tension. Allow your jaw to drop so your teeth aren't touching. Relax your lips, all mouth, and let the very base of your tongue relax.

Your whole body is relaxed now. Once again, scan it mentally with your attention. If you feel tension anywhere, put the intentional effort into relaxing that area.

Allow any stress remaining anywhere in your body to collect on the surface, from where you can let it go with the next breath out.

When our mind is under pressure, our body becomes tense. On the opposite, when our body is relaxed, it's a signal for the brain that everything's fine and safe to relax.

You are safe.
Everything is okay.
You are powerful.
It's safe to relax now.
You are relaxed.
All the stress has disappeared.

Your breathing is calm and deep.
Your body is completely relaxed.
It is turn on your mind to enjoy deep relaxation, rest, and recharge.

That's where all the stress is coming from.

We are used to creating numerous thoughts and follow most of them. So, our minds are overwhelmed by all sorts of worries, fears, to-do lists, and scenarios of what might happen. In a constant rush, our minds have o time to slow down and relax. Most health issues and conditions come from the mind. That's why it is crucial to learn how to soothe our minds and give them time to repair and recharge. Even the best personal assistants, as your brain is, need rest.
Accept the fact that there will always be some thoughts going through your mind. It's perfectly normal, and it's the mind's job to produce them. So, don't stress yourself about that.
Take a deep breath. Notice the first thought that is arising in your mind. Don't engage, don't follow it. Just notice it, and with breathing out, let it go.
Repeat this with the next one. Notice the thought forming in your mind. Take a deep breath. Exhale, and let it go.
Notice how thoughts are slowing down to accommodate the rhythm of your breathing.
Some of the thoughts are fast, like bouncing balls. Catch it, and hit it as far as you can. Some of them are a bit slower, like a big beach ball. Some of them are slow and floating, like balloons. Catch them gently just for a moment, and let float by. As you are going on with this practice, breathing, noticing, and letting go, you'll notice that your thoughts became slower and lighter. There will be fewer bouncing balls and more balloons.
Moreover, they will come to you so easy like soap balloons or feathers. Notice the feather floating to you. Just blow it away and watch it pass by.

Now, for each disturbing or negative thought, imagine a little dark cloud in the sky. Visualize you are lying on your back, watching the sky. The clouds have different dark shades and colors, depending on how stressful the thought is, from greyish to black.
Once all of your worries and stress are sent to the sky, it's time for relief. Watch your stressful thought and the dark cloud you created for them. Breathe in, and with breathing out, imagine you are releasing the stress and worries. While doing it, observe all the darkness is leaving the cloud. It is becoming lighter and lighter until it is entirely white and fluffy.

Skip to the next one. Breathe in, collecting all the stress and darkness. Breathe out, let go, and watch the cloud becoming snow white.
With the next breath, take up all the darkness from the next thought and cloud and breathe it out.
Do this for a while until all the clouds become white, light, and feathery. Feel ease. Enjoy the sensation of being free from stressful thoughts. They are not heavy nor dark anymore. Your burden became lighter and easier.
Now, take a deep breath, and breathing out, imagine you are blowing the first white cloud away. It flows away and disappears in the distance. There's clear blue now in the place where it used to be. Breathe in, and repeat with the next cloud. Breathe out and blow it away.
Do this for all the clouds.
There is a clear, blue sky with no clouds above you now. Your mind is clear, too. Enjoy this sense of calmness, easiness, and lightness. Your mind is relaxed now.
With your mind relaxed and calm, go back to focusing on your breathing.

With each breath, mentally say these affirmations to yourself:
I am calm. Breathe out.
Breathe in through your nose. I am relaxed. Breathe out through your mouth.
Breathe in. I feel at ease. Breathe out slowly.
I feel tranquility.
I am confident.
I am skilled.
I am focused.
Breathe in and say to yourself: I can handle anything that life brings to me. Breathe out.
There is peace within me.
Breathe in through your nose. I feel relaxed. Breathe out through your mouth.
I am intelligent.
I am calm.
I am wonderful.
I am relaxed now.
Take a deep breath. I make peace with everything outside and within me. Breathe out slowly.
I feel all the cells of my body are relaxed now.
I bring light and ease with me wherever I go.
I am powerful.
I can handle everything with ease.
Breathe in through your nose. I am in harmony. Breathe out.
I am calm. Breathe out.
Breathe in through your nose. I am relaxed. Breathe out through your mouth.
Breathe in. I feel at ease. Breathe out slowly.
I feel tranquility.
I am confident.
I am skilled.
I am focused.
Breathe in and say to yourself: I can handle anything that life brings to me. Breathe out.
There is peace within me.
Breathe in through your nose. I feel relaxed. Breathe out through your mouth.
I am intelligent.
I am calm.
I am wonderful.
I am relaxed now.
Take a deep breath. I make peace with everything outside and within me. Breathe out slowly.
I feel all the cells of my body are relaxed now.
I bring light and ease with me wherever I go.
I am powerful.
I can handle everything with ease.
Breathe in through your nose. I am in harmony. Breathe out.

Feel your body relaxed from head to toes. Feel the surface comfortably supporting you. Visualize a cloud forming beneath you. It's the size of your body, and it's the most comfortable place you've ever been to. It's supporting you perfectly, cradling your relaxed body, soft yet secure. Rest on this cloud. It's here only for you.

Now, feel the cloud slowly moves up. It elevates, taking you further and further from the ground. You know you are safe and secure, and you can rest on your cloud, even so high in the sky.

You can see the land. Everything seems so small from here. You can see places, mountains, rivers, fields. Everything seems like a colorful quilt. Now, look at all those things that used to provoke your stress. It's surprising how small and insignificant they look from here! All the troubles, worries, issues with health or finances, everything that bothered and stressed you out is left down there, and you can barely see it. Here, on your fluffy cloud, you feel no stress and have no worries: just relaxation and the feeling and ease.

Now, imagine a golden light suddenly starts to shine from the center of your cloud. It looks like a little Sun is hidden behind it. The light becomes stronger and stronger, and now the whole cloud shines brightly. You can feel the light is penetrating your body and spreading through it. Your feet glow, your whole legs shine. You can feel your stomach and chest shine with golden light. Your hands and arms also glow. Now your head is radiating the light. Your whole body shines. You can feel the light spreading on the inside, too, filling your heart and making your blood golden, too. The light is healing and relaxing. It's a cure for any stress. As you radiate it, you spread peace and calmness. It's everywhere, within and around you. It wraps and covers you, relaxing your thoughts, emotions, cells, organs, bones. It lights up any darkness and stress remaining anywhere within you. Have a bath in the golden light and enjoy resting in it. All the stress seems like a distant memory. You don't have to turn back to it ever again. You will always have this feeling to come back to. You can get on your cloud and rest in golden light, far away from everything that stresses you out.

You are completely relaxed now. All the stress is drained out of you. Your breathing is deep and slow, your mind is clear and calm, and your body is completely relaxed. Your cloud is back on the ground now. You can get up when you feel ready.

Gently open your eyes and slowly get back to your usual activity, completely refreshed, energized, and stress-free.

# Guided Meditation For Self-healing

50 min

Welcome to the meditation for self-healing. Its purpose is to remind your body of its natural abilities to heal itself.

Whether you don't feel well or you have some serious diagnose, this meditation will help you.

You'll feel better immediately after finishing it, and, with everyday use, you'll notice unbelievable improvement in your health.

There is a divine power within you, the same one that created you, and that can heal you even from worst conditions. Human bodies have the ability to repair themselves and to achieve perfect balance. When we are not in balance, illnesses occur. The process works in the opposite direction as well, so if you manage to bring back perfect harmony, health issues disappear.
However, to heal themselves, your body and mind need some peace and quiet time. If you are in a constant rush, always active, tensed, never completely relaxed and tranquil, your body can't repair itself. That's why meditation is the perfect way to enable self-healing. Your body has its own wisdom, and you don't need to teach it anything. You just need to move from the way and allow it to do its job. Your busy mind is the one who needs to be calmed so the natural processes can go on undisturbedly.
In this meditation, we'll do all that is needed to remind your body of how to heal itself, and everything to allow it to do that. You will learn how to relax the whole body, calm mind, slow and deepen breathing, show appreciation, and love to your body, and remind it of its natural powers.

You can do this meditation whenever you like, during day or night. For the best results, I recommend you do it as often as possible. Find a quiet place where you won't be disturbed for about an hour. This is the time only for you and your healing. Make it a priority. Turn off any ringers, all notifications, and all distractors. Choose the most comfortable position. I recommend practicing it in a lying position, but choose whatever is most convenient. For the best experience, use earphones.
Place your attention to my voice. It will guide you to a deeper, relaxed state from which you can empower your body to heal itself, and engage in your healing process.
Make yourself comfortable. The temperature should be pleasant, not too warm, nor cold. Your back should be straight, your legs straight, slightly apart, and hands straight beside your body. Slowly calm before the meditation begins.
Try to calm and slow your breathing. Exhales longer than inhales are the sign for your body to relax. Breathe in through the nose, to the count of four. One, two, three, four. Breathe out through the mouth to the count of eight. One, two, three, four, five, six, seven, eight.
Repeat it. Breathe in. One, two, three, four. Breathe out. One, two, three, four, five, six, seven, eight.
Do it once again. Inhale - one, two, three, four.
Exhale - one, two, three, four, five, six, seven, eight.
If you can't reach those numbers, don't worry. Do what you can without forcing yourself.
Being gentle to yourself is now a priority.
Now, allow your breathing to drop back to its natural rhythm.
With every breath in, imagine you are inhaling white, healing light. With each exhale, let go of everything you want to let go. Negative emotions are like a poison inside you. Let them go.

Inhale white light.
Exhale tension.
Inhale light. Exhale anger.
Inhale light. Exhale anxiety.
Inhale healing. Exhale resentment.
Inhale light. Exhale hatred.
Do this for a while, until you let go of all negativity you've been holding inside.

It's time to relax your body now. From the relaxed state, you can talk to your body, send it love and appreciation, and help it activate its natural healing power. When you relax completely, you move your consciousness from the way, and your body is free to repair.
Breathing slowly and deeply, bring your attention to your toes and feet. Feel the aliveness in them. Tense your feet, and then allow them to loosen. Relax the whole feet, from toes to heels. Relax your ankles. Tense the muscles of your lower legs. Hold them tensed for a moment. Three, two, one, and relax. Relax your knees. Place your focus on your thighs. Feel the backside of your thighs on the surface. Tense the muscles of your thighs. Hold it for three, two, one, and relax. Allow your legs to open up a bit to the ceiling. Tense your glutes as tight as you can. Hold for a moment, three, two, one, and relax. Allow your glutes, hips, and pelvic area to relax. Take a breath in, and breathing out, relax your lower body a bit more. Do it a few times. Feel the relaxation and ease spreading through your lower body, and it becomes heavier, sinking in the surface.
Your hands are lying straight beside your body, with your palms up. Feel the aliveness in them. Bring your attention to the sensations in your fingers. Stretch and tense them for a moment, and then relax. Relax your palms, hands, and wrists. Move your attention up to your forearms. Tense them to the count of three, two, one, and then relax. Relax your elbows. Move up to your upper arms. Tense the muscles, and hold them tight for a moment. Then allow them to loosen. Your whole hands and arms are relaxed, from very fingertips to your shoulders.
Notice the movements of your stomach, as it moves up and down in the rhythm of your breathing. Pull your navel to the spine and tense the abdominals. Hold them tight for three, two, one. And relax.
Take a nice, deep breath, fill your chest, and tense them. Breathe out, and allow your chest muscles to loosen. Feel the relaxed feeling in your stomach and chest.
Bring your awareness to your back. Feel the surface below, supporting it. Tense all of your back muscles. Breathe in, and with the breath out, relax your lower back. Inhale deeply again, and exhale, relaxing the middle part of your back. Move your attention up, and with the next exhale, relax your upper back. Feel your back is loosened and relax, sinking into the surface. Feel the lightness, as you were floating yet been strongly supported.

Now, tense your shoulders as firmly as you can, so they can almost touch your ears. Then, with the exhale, allow them to drop and relax. Feel the muscles of your shoulders loosen and become soft and elastic. With each exhale, your shoulders become more and more relaxed. With your shoulders relaxing, the whole body becomes relaxed. Feel the relief, calmness, and peace in your body.
Tense your neck by pushing your jaw to your chest. Then bring your head back and relax your neck. Bring your awareness to your throat. With the next exhale, allow your throat to relax and open. Clench your jaw. Then release it, allowing it to drop down. Tense your facial muscles, and then relax them, one by one. Relax your cheeks, the eye muscles, your lips, and tongue. Raise your eyebrows and tense the forehead and the scalp. With breath out, allow them to relax. Relax the back and the top of your head. Feel its weight, and your head being cradled by the surface.
 Your whole body is completely relaxed now. Feel the ease and tranquility. Breathe deeply and slowly, and enjoy these moments of deep relaxation. Your organs, systems, your blood, bones, and cells are

relaxing now. They are all regenerating and healing. There's so much happening within your body right now. Appreciate those moments of deep reenergizing rest.

How often do you tell your body how thankful you are for everything it does for you? It is time to let it know how grateful you are.

Mentally say „thank you" to your feet and legs for holding you and taking you wherever you want to go. It's such a blessing to be able to walk and change places. Thank your glutes for supporting you while you are sitting. Thank your genitals and reproductive organs for bringing you joy and possibilities to reproduce yourself. Thank your urinary and digestive systems for cleaning your body and getting rid of everything you don't need anymore. Mentally say thank you to your stomach for digesting food for you, enabling you to use nutrients. Show appreciation to your lungs for making you breathe and use the air, which keeps you alive. Thank your back for supporting you, holding you up and straight. Say „thank you" to your hands for doing so many things for you - for holding, bringing, carrying, hugging, creating, and so much more they do for you. Thank your neck for holding and moving your head. Too often, we don't notice these „workers" within our body, and we are not aware of how blessed we are to be able to move, to breathe, to walk, to see. Acknowledge your blessings. Thank your brain for doing such a magnificent job of thinking for you and managing all the activities within your body. It's such a great manager! Thank your mouth for enabling you to express yourself, to communicate, to feel the taste of the food you eat, to kiss those you love. Say „thank you" to your nose and to your eyes. It's a precious gift being able to see. You can see colors, the faces, the stars glowing in the dark. Feel appreciation so deep to fill the whole of your being. If you count all of your blessings, it's not surprising even if you begin to cry from happiness and gratefulness.

There's no better cure in the world than love. Love can heal everything. So, show your body how much you love it. Pour love in each part of it.

Again, start from your feet. Mentally say them, „I love you." Move up, sending your love to your legs, your hips, glutes. Feel the love for your belly and chest. Your back also needs to hear, „I love you." Pour love into your hands and arms. Say „I love you" to your shoulders and neck. Then, pour love into your head. Mentally say to your body, „I love you. You are great. You can do amazing things. I pour love in every part of you." Pour love in every organ, every muscle, and bone. Pour so much love in each cell as it can hold, so every cell of your body becomes a tiny star that spreads the love around. Your body is full of love now. Your organs work cheerfully—your blood flows in the cheerful rhythm. You are bathing in self-love. It cures everything. It repairs, rejuvenates, and heals everything that needed to be fixed. If there is some part of your body that needs your special attention, pour some extra love in that place. The infinite and unconditional love is spreading from your heart.

You are in a state of deep relaxation. Your breathing is slow and deep. Your body is full of divine, infinite love that is healing it. From this point, you can talk to it, to empower the process of self-healing.

Remind your body of its natural power to heal itself and restore balance, and show it your trust.

You can mentally repeat or just listen to what I am saying.

Body, I love you. You are perfect, just the way you are.

I pour love into you.

You deserve to be perfectly healthy.

You are meant to be balanced and work as a wholeness.

Health is your inborn right.

You are wise.

You have the ability to heal yourself, and you know how to do that.

I trust you and encourage you to do that.

I allow you to do whatever it takes to heal.

You don't need help, just my trust, and support, and I am giving it to you now.

I allow the divine power within you to guide me and to bring you back to your natural state of harmony.

I listen to you, I understand you and appreciate what you have to tell me. Now, I know you do that because you need my attention.

I let go of everything that stands on the way to healing.

I'm ready to let go of any negative emotions, limiting beliefs, and holding stubbornly to anything. You know the best what's best for you.

You know the way, and I trust you.

Heal yourself, heal every cell, and every organ within you, make everything do in a perfect way, because I love you, you are amazing, and you deserve to be healthy and happy.

I know you have everything you need for healing, and you will do that perfectly in a way that is best for you.

Now, visualize, you are in front of a massive, golden gate. You push it, and the door opens. You are stepping into a beautiful garden. It's full of green; there are high trees, flowers, and grass. It's silent, and you can hear only birds and insects. The sunlight is shining through the crowns. As you are stepping down the path, you can hear the sound of water. You still can't see any water, but you can hear it. So, you move on down the path in the direction from where the sound is coming.

This garden is huge. Finally, in front of you, there's a marble pergola. That's where the sound is coming from. Coming closer, you can see a pool there. The water is crystal clear, sparkling. You know that is healing water, that helps the body to remind of its self-healing power. You sit on the side of the pool, with your feet in the water. On your surprise, your feet start shining. You decide to get into the water. It's only waist-deep at this side of the pool. You're looking at your legs, and you can see they are glimmering. The feeling is as if the water is massaging your feet, legs, and hips. With each step forward, it's a bit deeper. You are moving on, enjoying the feeling, and knowing that healing is happening right now. Finally, you dive in and feel the water wrapping you. It's above your head, and your whole body is sparkling with glimmering shine.

Getting out the water, you feel renewed and refreshed as if it washed off everything you needed to shake off.

Your body is reminded of its powers and abilities to heal. It's full of energy and strength. You know the healing process is already going on.

Besides the pergola, there's an outdoor daybed with canopy. You didn't notice it at first. You know it's here for you. So, you lye down and make yourself comfortable. You can feel a soft breeze on your skin and the comfort of the mattress. You can hear the water sound and feel the smell of fresh grass.

Your whole body is relaxed, rejuvenated, and full of fresh energy. You breathe deeply, knowing a new part of the healing process is about to begin.

Take a deep breath in and imagine a healing, golden light entering your feet. With the breath out, notice your feet are shining brightly.

Breathe in and feel the light entering your muscles and bones of your lower legs. Breathe out, and visualize your legs shining with golden light. Breathe the light in your upper legs, allowing it to fill your thighs and hips. Your hips and whole legs are shining with golden light. On the inhale, fill the light entering your pelvic area, and on the exhale, see the bright light radiating from your glutes and pelvis. Breathe the healing light filling your stomach. Breathing out, see the bright light spreading from your center.

Inhale the healing light and fill your chest. Exhale, and feel your chest shining.

Breathe the golden light through your spine and allow it to spread all over your back. The golden light is entering every muscle of your back. Breathe out. Your back is shining. It seems as if you are lying on the shiny star.

Breathing in, imagine the light entering your fingers and spreading through your hands. The golden light is filling your lower and upper arms. Breathing out, notice your arms and hands shining gold.

The golden light is moving up to your shoulders, and they shine. With the next breath in, your neck and head are filling with the healing, golden light. Exhaling, notice your head is shining brightly.

The light is entering through your skin, wrapping your organs, penetrating all bones, and muscle tissues. Your cells are shining, bathing in golden, healing light.

While your body is healing, bathing in golden light, using divine wisdom and its natural powers to heal, you can empower it by sending love, blessings, and positive, supportive thoughts.

Take a nice, deep breath. Breathe out slowly.

When ready, gently open your eyes. You can move on with your day, feeling fresh and reenergized. Or, if you want, let yourself drift off to sleep, and have nice dreams.

# Affirmations for self-healing

60 min

To heal yourself, you need to change some thinking patterns that brought you there.
Listen to these affirmations and repeat them mentally or out loud. They will become your new, supportive beliefs and help you perfect health you deserve.
I am strong and powerful
I have the power to heal.
My body and mind are healing now.
Life is supporting me.
The Universe is holding my back.
I love myself, unconditionally.
I choose health.
I deserve to be perfectly healthy. That is my natural right.
I am ready to forgive and let go.
I am full of energy.
I am thankful for my positive, healthy thoughts.
I am grateful for the perfect balance of my body and mind.
All of my cells are healthy and vibrant.
I am grateful for my body and its wisdom.
I am complete.
I am whole.
I feel great and full of energy.
I allow my body and mind to heal.
I love life, and life loves me. It has a lot to give me, and I am ready to experience it.
I am in perfect harmony and in peace with the world. I allow divine energy and higher intelligence to guide my body and heal it.
I have the power to heal.
I am strong and powerful.

My body and mind are healing now.
I deserve to be perfectly healthy. That is my natural right.
I am ready to forgive and let go.
Life is supporting me.
The Universe is holding my back.
I love myself, unconditionally.
I choose health.
I am full of energy.
All of my cells are healthy and vibrant.
I am grateful for my body and its wisdom.
I am thankful for my positive, healthy thoughts.
I am grateful for the perfect balance of my body and mind.
I am complete.
I am whole.
I feel great and full of energy.

I allow my body and mind to heal.
I love life, and life loves me. It has a lot to give me, and I am ready to experience it.
I am in perfect harmony and in peace with the world. I allow divine energy and higher intelligence to guide my body and heal it.
I have the power to heal.
I am strong and powerful.

My body and mind are healing now.
I deserve to be perfectly healthy. That is my natural right.
I am ready to forgive and let go.
Life is supporting me.
The Universe is holding my back.
I love myself, unconditionally.
I choose health.
I am full of energy.
All of my cells are healthy and vibrant.
I am grateful for my body and its wisdom.
I am thankful for my positive, healthy thoughts.
I am grateful for the perfect balance of my body and mind.
I am complete.
I am whole.
I feel great and full of energy.
I allow my body and mind to heal.
I love life, and life loves me. It has a lot to give me, and I am ready to experience it.
I am in perfect harmony and in peace with the world. I allow divine energy and higher intelligence to guide my body and heal it.
I have the power to heal.
I am strong and powerful.

My body and mind are healing now.
I deserve to be perfectly healthy. That is my natural right.
I am ready to forgive and let go.
Life is supporting me.
The Universe is holding my back.
I love myself, unconditionally.
I choose health.
I am full of energy.
All of my cells are healthy and vibrant.
I am grateful for my body and its wisdom.
I am thankful for my positive, healthy thoughts.
I am grateful for the perfect balance of my body and mind.
I am complete.
I am whole.
I feel great and full of energy.
I allow my body and mind to heal.
I love life, and life loves me. It has a lot to give me, and I am ready to experience it.
I am in perfect harmony and in peace with the world. I allow divine energy and higher intelligence to guide my body and heal it.

I have the power to heal.
I am strong and powerful.

My body and mind are healing now.
I deserve to be perfectly healthy. That is my natural right.
I am ready to forgive and let go.
Life is supporting me.
The Universe is holding my back.
I love myself, unconditionally.
I choose health.
I am full of energy.
All of my cells are healthy and vibrant.
I am grateful for my body and its wisdom.
I am thankful for my positive, healthy thoughts.
I am grateful for the perfect balance of my body and mind.
I am complete.
I am whole.
I feel great and full of energy.
I allow my body and mind to heal.
I love life, and life loves me. It has a lot to give me, and I am ready to experience it.
I am in perfect harmony and in peace with the world. I allow divine energy and higher intelligence to guide my body and heal it.

# Meditation for Rapid Weight Loss

30 min

Welcome to the meditation for rapid weight loss. I recommend you practice it for twenty-one days in a row, for the best results.
Choose the time and a place when you won't be disturbed.
Make yourself comfortable in a sitting or a lying position.
You are completely safe. If you want to open your eyes, you can do it whenever you want.
This is the time just for you to relax, let go, and feel good.
Let's get your body relaxed, and your mind focused.
To get what you want, you need to appreciate what you already have first.
We'll reprogram your subconsciousness, so you feel good now.
Take a deep breath in, breathe out and allow yourself to feel relaxed.
Listen to the sound of my voice and allow it to take you deeper.
You can close your eyes or keep them open, as you wish. If you wish, close your eyes now. Let go and relax. It feels so good to close your eyes and let them relax.
Take a deep breath. Let it out again and feel relaxed; focus on your breath, breathe deeper and slower with each breath.
On the inhale, filling your lungs, and on the exhale, breathing out old, still air. Breathe in positive energy. With each breath, your mind slows down a bit more.
As your mind slows down, you are going even deeper with relaxation.
If your mind wanders, it's okay. If thoughts are running through your mind, it's okay too. Let them disappear like clouds in the sky.
If you start to feel sleepy, that's okay, too. Just breathe and relax, comfort your feelings.
Now, mentally scan your body, notice the parts where you might feel tensed or uncomfortable. Breathe deep and relax that area, letting go of discomfort. Just listen to my voice and try to visualize. Let me guide you on this journey. You are creating what you want with ease. You are allowing your mind, body, and spirit to be together and work together.
Open your mind to positive energy.
Take a few moments to appreciate all the good in your life. Feel the gratitude and allow positive energy to flow through you. As you're in this state, you are creating a new, motivated attitude. Your subconscious will keep it for those moments when you lack motivation.
Your choices define who you are. Now you choose to make healthy and proactive choices, taking charge of your life and the future.
It's time to be proactive now. You'll begin to see opportunities that you didn't see before. You strive for happiness and success. You'll find fulfillment, living in the now, being positive, and keeping a happy attitude. You are in the present, choosing to take steps every day for your highest good.
Be who you want to be and live the life you want. Your ambitions and wishes are at your fingertips. Breathing deeper and deeper, you are reaching it now. You are making your life happen. This is the perfect state to start your date. You give yourself attitude and energy to achieve whatever you want. You are in the right place, doing the right thing, just by listening to this.
Now, I'm going to countdown backward. When we get to one, you'll be on a level from where you can retrain your brain. If you can't remember what I say, don't worry. Your subconsciousness will do everything for you.
Take a deep breath. Breathe out. Breathe in deeply, and let it out.

Five. You are open to positive energy. Your brain is taking everything I'm saying.
Four. You are open, and you listen, ready and open on a new level. You are ready to make a positive change.
Three. You are relaxed down, down, deeper, and deeper. You are creating powerful, positive thoughts. Let go of any tension.
Two. You feel deeply relaxed, going deeper and deeper.
One. You are absolutely relaxed. You feel positive, motivated, comfortable. Your thoughts are positive. It feels so good. Let yourself enjoy this relaxation on the deepest level.
Your mind is now open, ready. As you relax, you know there are so many good things in your life now. You have so many blessings and reasons to celebrate.
Feel the Universe is hugging you, supporting and loving you.
The Universe lets the positive energy flow through your body, like a warm, glowing light lifting you up. It makes you feel safe and secure.
You are complete and perfect. You are taking action. You are strong and powerful. You will achieve your greatness.
You are going deeper and deeper, breathing deep and slow. It feels so good to let go and relax.

It's time to make positive decisions and changes.
Giving up is not an option. Your health depends on these choices and changes. Your mind and body will absorb a lot of benefits from your different choices during the day. Use your freedom to make choices for your highest good.

Hunger is a state of mind. If you reduce intake, you will surely feel the effects. When you feel discomfort, you don't have to take food to feel better. Stay committed to the path that you chose.
Listen to these affirmations, and your mind will change the self-image, improve your mobility and health overall.

Relax, listening to these affirmations, seeing your body in its best shape.

I am slim and fit.
I always make healthy choices for myself.
I am motivated to lose weight.
I'm dedicated to following my weight loss plan.
I am disciplined in my eating habits.
I am strong in mind and body.
I am completely focused on losing weight.
I am beginning to lose weight.
I live a healthy lifestyle, and it's easy for me.
Others are noticing I am losing weight.
It's easy for me to lose weight.
I always choose healthy over junk food.
I am disciplined.
I respect my body.
I take care of my body.
I find it easy to lose weight.
I am naturally slim.
I believe in my ability to lose weight and keep it off.
I deserve to be slim, healthy, and happy.
I have a naturally healthy mind and body.

I naturally lose weight.
I think positively.
It's easy to stay in shape.
I love to nurture my body.
I have a great, strong, slim body.
I am slim and beautiful.
I visualize my ideal body, and I'm dedicated to making it happen.
I become thinner and healthier.
I am focused on achieving my weight loss goals.
I'm becoming fitter and fitter.
I reach my health goals.
I'm becoming more focused on losing weight.
I am losing weight.
Others notice I am losing weight.
I am closer and closer to my ideal body.
I am transforming into a slim, healthy, and happy person.
I am motivated to lose weight.
I stick to my exercising plan.
I am motivated to be the healthiest I could be.
I enjoy exercising every day.
I am more and more motivated.
It comes naturally to me.
I love losing weight.
I am focused on getting my ideal weight.
I love keeping myself in perfect shape.
I eat regularly.
I eat lots of fruits and vegetables.
I always eat a balanced meal.
I always eat breakfast.
I eat healthy to energize my mind and body.
I am focused on nurturing my body properly.
I am starting to eat smaller meals.
I always choose healthy foods.
I enjoy eating fruit and vegetables.
I am a naturally healthy eater.
I love vegetables.
I love fruit.
I have complete control over my diet.
I enjoy eating healthy foods.
Nutrition is important for my quality of life.
I have a fast metabolism.
My metabolic rate is increasing.
I am a calorie-burning machine.
I burn calories quickly.
I am burning calories faster and faster each day.
I focus my mind on increasing my metabolic rate.
I enjoy dieting.
I have a healthy relationship with food.
I respect my body.

I love my body.
I have a healthy body image.
I accept myself completely.
Each day I feel and look better.
I am grateful for my body.
I am slim and fit.
I take care of my body.
I am motivated to become healthy.
I choose healthy food.
I am slim and fit.
I always make healthy choices for myself.
I am motivated to lose weight.
I'm dedicated to following my weight loss plan.
I am disciplined in my eating habits.
I am strong in mind and body.
I am completely focused on losing weight.
I am beginning to lose weight.
I live a healthy lifestyle, and it's easy for me.
Others are noticing I am losing weight.
It's easy for me to lose weight.
I always choose healthy over junk food.
I am disciplined.
I respect my body.
I take care of my body.
I find it easy to lose weight.
I am naturally slim.
I believe in my ability to lose weight and keep it off.
I deserve to be slim, healthy, and happy.
I have a naturally healthy mind and body.
I naturally lose weight.
I think positively.
It's easy to stay in shape.
I love to nurture my body.
I have a great, strong, slim body.
I am slim and beautiful.
I visualize my ideal body, and I'm dedicated to making it happen.
I become thinner and healthier.
I am focused on achieving my weight loss goals.
I'm becoming fitter and fitter.
I reach my health goals.
I'm becoming more focused on losing weight.
I am losing weight.
Others notice I am losing weight.
I am closer and closer to my ideal body.
I am transforming into a slim, healthy, and happy person.
I am motivated to lose weight.
I stick to my exercising plan.
I am motivated to be the healthiest I could be.
I enjoy exercising every day.

I am more and more motivated.
It comes naturally to me.
I love losing weight.
I am focused on getting my ideal weight.
I love keeping myself in perfect shape.
I eat regularly.
I eat lots of fruits and vegetables.
I always eat a balanced meal.
I always eat breakfast.
I eat healthy to energize my mind and body.
I am focused on nurturing my body properly.
I am starting to eat smaller meals.
I always choose healthy foods.
I enjoy eating fruit and vegetables.
I am a naturally healthy eater.
I love vegetables.
I love fruit.
I have complete control over my diet.
I enjoy eating healthy foods.
Nutrition is important for my quality of life.
I have a fast metabolism.
My metabolic rate is increasing.
I am a calorie-burning machine.
I burn calories quickly.
I am burning calories faster and faster each day.
I focus my mind on increasing my metabolic rate.
I enjoy dieting.
I have a healthy relationship with food.
I respect my body.
I love my body.
I have a healthy body image.
I accept myself completely.
Each day I feel and look better.
I am grateful for my body.
I am slim and fit.
I take care of my body.
I am motivated to become healthy.
I choose healthy food.
I am slim and fit.
I always make healthy choices for myself.
I am motivated to lose weight.
I'm dedicated to following my weight loss plan.
I am disciplined in my eating habits.
I am strong in mind and body.
I am completely focused on losing weight.
I am beginning to lose weight.
I live a healthy lifestyle, and it's easy for me.
Others are noticing I am losing weight.
It's easy for me to lose weight.

I always choose healthy over junk food.
I am disciplined.
I respect my body.
I take care of my body.
I find it easy to lose weight.
I am naturally slim.
I believe in my ability to lose weight and keep it off.
I deserve to be slim, healthy, and happy.
I have a naturally healthy mind and body.
I naturally lose weight.
I think positively.
It's easy to stay in shape.
I love to nurture my body.
I have a great, strong, slim body.
I am slim and beautiful.
I visualize my ideal body, and I'm dedicated to making it happen.
I become thinner and healthier.
I am focused on achieving my weight loss goals.
I'm becoming fitter and fitter.
I reach my health goals.
I'm becoming more focused on losing weight.
I am losing weight.
Others notice I am losing weight.
I am closer and closer to my ideal body.
I am transforming into a slim, healthy, and happy person.
I am motivated to lose weight.
I stick to my exercising plan.
I am motivated to be the healthiest I could be.
I enjoy exercising every day.
I am more and more motivated.
It comes naturally to me.
I love losing weight.
I am focused on getting my ideal weight.
I love keeping myself in perfect shape.
I eat regularly.
I eat lots of fruits and vegetables.
I always eat a balanced meal.
I always eat breakfast.
I eat healthy to energize my mind and body.
I am focused on nurturing my body properly.
I am starting to eat smaller meals.
I always choose healthy foods.
I enjoy eating fruit and vegetables.
I am a naturally healthy eater.
I love vegetables.
I love fruit.
I have complete control over my diet.
I enjoy eating healthy foods.
Nutrition is important for my quality of life.

I have a fast metabolism.
My metabolic rate is increasing.
I am a calorie-burning machine.
I burn calories quickly.
I am burning calories faster and faster each day.
I focus my mind on increasing my metabolic rate.
I enjoy dieting.
I have a healthy relationship with food.
I respect my body.
I love my body.
I have a healthy body image.
I accept myself completely.
Each day I feel and look better.
I am grateful for my body.
I am slim and fit.
I take care of my body.
I am motivated to become healthy.
I choose healthy food.
I always make choices for my highest good.
Take a nice, deep breathe. Follow my voice as I am counting. When we come to five, gently open your eyes.
One. Take a breath in. Breathe out.
Two. Breathe in. Breathe out.
Three. Breathe on. Breathe out.
Four. Breathe in. Breathe out.
Breathe in once again. Breathe out, and open your eyes.
Go on with your usual activities, making the best choices for your health during the day.

# Guided Meditation For Overthinking

30 min

Welcome to the guided meditation for stop overthinking.
This guided meditation session is aimed to help you finally release yourself from overthinking and create peace in your inner space. It will also help you learn how to calm your mind, training it to observe more and engage less.
It is designed to help you free yourself from the constant, useless mental activity and tendency of your mind to be busy all the time. This practice will help you gain significant insights and notice the thinking patterns that don't serve you, so you can end them and positively benefit in all ways.
Please, listen to this meditation only when you can safely bring your full awareness to your complete comfort and relaxation.
Probably you've noticed that sometimes your thoughts can build up so much that you can't stop them anymore. They become a constant mental chatter that causes you stress and anxiety. Our minds are used to be busy all the time with unhelpful mental activity. Your mind might have developed habits of worrying all the time, analyzing, and evaluating personal events over and over again. It needs problems to solve, so it seeks them no matter where. You might feel trapped or locked in an endless spiral of thinking without the possibility to stop. These thinking patterns are mot often connected to chronic anxiety and depression. Fortunately, there is an exit from this thinking spiral, and you can find relief from this rumination. The solution is never to think more. The key is the opposite - stepping out of your head. Focusing on physical sensation and learning how to be truly present in here and now will help you stop the unwanted thinking—practicing mindfulness meditation will teach you how to do that.
With these simple techniques, you'll learn how to train your conscious mind to focus on more productive things, turn from useless mental activity to enjoying sensations, be consciously present, and change the emotional response.
Let us begin.
Choose a time in a day when you can focus just on relaxation and won't be disturbed for a while. Find a comfortable place where you can be alone, listen, and enjoy inner silence.
Find a comfortable position and posture. You can sit or lie down; just be sure that nothing's drawing your attention. Your back should be straightened, and all the muscles in an effortless position.
Once you find the best posture, bring your attention inward. Focus on your breathing. Don't try to control or hold your breath; just observe it and be aware of each breath.
Notice everything you can about it. Notice the cool air entering your nostrils and going down, through your airwaves, to the lungs and stomach. Notice your stomach and chest rise and fall in the rhythm of your breathing. Become aware of the muscles engaging. Be aware of your ribs expanding and contracting with each breath. Feel the air all the way back to your nose and out. No need to control it nor change anything; just breathe in your natural rhythm, and observe, letting go of the need to control.
 Now, become aware of the temperature of your body. Notice the warmth and coolness. Some parts of your body might be warmer than others. That's normal for all the resting bodies.
Acknowledge any sensations of warmth in your hands and fingers. Notice the warmth or coolness in your feet and toes. Notice any sensations of warmth in your legs and arms. And any sensation of warmth in the center of your body.
Just become aware of these sensations and acknowledge they're perfectly normal. Accept them, and allow yourself to stay with them for a moment.

As your body relaxes, you might notice some movements. Acknowledge them without forcing your body to be totally still. Be aware of all the movements of the body. Notice that some parts may feel more relaxed than others, while some may feel tension or tightness. And it's alright. You don't have to force partial relaxation. For now, it's enough to acknowledge those sensations. Just allow your mind to observe and accept everything for what it is. You don't have to do a thing. You don't have to think nor control anything. Allow yourself to be at your normal pace. You don't have to rush anywhere. You are at the right place, at the right time. You don't need to be anywhere else. This is the time just for you, your relaxation, and for gaining a better self-understanding.

Meditation will help you learn about yourself and get to know yourself better. You'll better understand your reactions, behaviors, and you'll grow the ability just to observe and accept things for what they are, to be fully aware and present.

As you continue to breathe consciously, you are fully present in here and now.

If you want to, you can slow your breathing now. Allow your next breath-in to be just a little slower and your next breath-out to become just a bit longer.

Slowing your cycles of breathing, you're sending signals to your mind to slow down. As feedback to that simple thought, your body and mind are gently slowing. It feels so good to calm your mind. Notice you don't have any excessive thought. You are not using too much thinking energy. You are simply thinking normally and naturally, asking your body to slow down and calm breath. Notice your slow breathing. It's easy and effortless. As you extend your awareness, bringing your focus to breathing, you feel relaxed and fully present.

As you observe each breath and your mental space is clear, you can notice every thought which arises. Just observe thoughts your mind wishes to create. It might be internal judgments, evaluations, a label, a phrase, a word or an image, any kind of distractions. Sometimes it may be a description. Your mind is not used to be quiet. It has a need to do something, at least, to describe or name things. Just note whatever it is that your mind wants to create. Become aware of the temporary nature of thinking.

Thoughts come, and thoughts go.

You always have a choice - to follow them or let them go. Instead of following each of them, choose to remain just a little further removed. You are allowing yourself to stay outside of evaluations, outside of mind's judgments, and instead, simply be, noticing these creations of the mind. Allow any thought that arises just to exist there. There is no need to try to control thinking. There's no need to try to change thoughts or thinking. Simply acknowledge the thoughts, allow them to be there for a while, and give them space to play.

Instead of an effort to control your thoughts, acceptance and allowance will make such thoughts come and go whenever they want and eventually fade away.

Yes, those thoughts are yours, but you also know and understand that who you are is much more than simply your thoughts.

You can witness the sparks of thoughts come and go, almost like shooting stars across a clear night sky. As a single thought come into your mind, you can easily notice it carries its own certain energy. Some thoughts have particularly strong energy and call for attention. Some are quieter.

But always, you can stay outside all of them, observant, resting, and relaxing.

From a comfortable distance, you can witness and watch as each thought arises and simply passes. Calm and observant in each moment, you can choose to turn your focus and awareness inwards, back to your breathing, breathing in and breathing out, always able to return to this focus on your breath.

Now allow this awareness to note and observe small sensations that come with each breath. This way, you are training your observant mind. Notice cool air as it enters your nostrils, passes through your nose, and becomes slightly warmer as it moves down through your airwaves. Feel it enters your lungs.

There's no need to hold a breath. Just remain mindful and observe your natural breathing cycles, allowing your body to breathe deeply and completely in its natural rhythm. Don't try to control it; just remain silent watcher observing each breath.

This technique is the basic mindful breath awareness. This practice is a powerful technique. By allowing yourself to focus on breathing this way simply, you can gently guide and return your conscious awareness always back to your breath.

As you allow individual thoughts to enter into your observation, however, wherever or whenever they arise, you are offering them your calmest acknowledge. You allow them to pass by, and their energy fades or burnout or disappear. You can let them pass by, offering no resistance.

You can observe who you really are and always remains. You are much more than your thoughts. You're observing, calmly detaching yourself. You calm yourself, always remaining in the present moment.

You are gaining the understanding that you are more than your thinking and your reactions.

There's always one more part of you, always observing, watching, and witnessing. And you are easily able to return always back to your breath, making a choice to remain present in the present, coming back to the breath, breathing in and breathing out.

You are consciously present now. Your mind is peaceful.

You can remain in this mindful state for as long as you wish.

If you wish, you can drift off to sleep from here. Or, otherwise, you may choose to remain awake and alert, calmly observing your breathing for as long as you want.

When you are ready, slowly open your eyes, get up, and go on with your usual activities, aware that you can always come back to this state of complete mindfulness.

# Guided Meditation To Stop Overthinking 2

30 min

Welcome. This guided meditation is aimed to help you finally stop excessive thinking. You can use it whenever you feel the need to soothe your mind and find relief from rushing thoughts.
Sit or lie down and make yourself comfortable. I recommend you use earphones for a more enjoyable experience.
Breathe deeply, and focus mainly on exhales.
Bring awareness to breathing. With each breath out, permit yourself to relax a bit more. Breathe deeply, with your abdominal muscles include.
Bring attention to your feet. Relax your feet.
Relax your toes, heels, whole feet.
Relax your ankles.
Feel a relaxed sensation in your ankles.
Focus on your lower legs, and intentionally relax them. The front and the backside of your lower legs - completely relaxed.
You still breathe deeply, with the focus on your breath-outs.
Relax your knees. Relax your thighs, the front and the backside of your thighs.
Your toes, heels, and feet are relaxed. Ankles - relaxed. Your lower legs, knees, and upper legs - relaxed.
Bring awareness to your glutes, your hips. Relax them. Feel your glutes relaxes and the whole lower half of the body. With every breath-out, your glutes are more relaxed.
Concentrate on your palms and hands. Relax your hands. Let your fingers relax. Relax your wrists.
Breathing deeply, you're concentrating on the exhales.
Relax your arms. Allow your elbows to loosen. Relax your upper arms. Your fingers, palms, wrists, whole hands - relaxed. Your lower arms, elbows, and upper arms - all relaxed.
Bring awareness to your stomach and chest. Breathing deeply, relax your stomach and chest.
Concentrate on your lower back. Feel the muscles of the lower back. Relax the lower back, and let this relaxed sensation move upwards, to your shoulders.
Allow your shoulders to relax. That is the key point in relaxation. Feel the relief. With each breath-out, your shoulders are more relaxed. Even when you think you relaxed them completely, you can relax them a bit more.
Observe your whole body is more relaxed as you're relaxing your shoulders.
Let your neck relax. Relax the back of your head. Allow your cheeks and your forehead to relax. Relax your ears.
Relax your mouth and jaw, let it loose. Calm and relax your eyes. Relax all those tiny eye muscles.
It's normal to have thoughts. It's natural. Don't resist them, don't try to fight them. Just acknowledge them and choose which of them you want to engage in.
The main purpose of this meditation is to create your safe place, your peaceful room, where you can enter whenever you want to rest and calm your mind.
Imagine your mind as a large house, with separated rooms inside. You have a particular room for each segment of your life – for work, family, health, relationships, a room for your finances, one for love, you name it. Also, imagine you havea separated room for your worries and problems. Now, step into one of the rooms. It's loud, full of thoughts and worries. Enter that room and observe which thoughts are there. Observe them, listen to them. You can notice one thing - those are not your thoughts; they belong to the

room. You just entered it. It's full of thoughts and worries. How do you feel while watching and listening to those thoughts? Which emotions do they provoke? Do you feel worried, stressed, frightened?

Now, exit that room. Now, you're going to your room. It's pure white. It's a room without thoughts. You can see yourself entering that room - white, bright, clean, and airy. Open the door and enter the peace. There's nothing else. It's absolutely quiet there. Observe your body now.

Observe the emotions you feel while being in that white room. Feel the peace filling your body and mind. That is your safe place from now on.

Stay there for a while, absolutely conscious, aware that it is the room without any thoughts. Acknowledge the peace and silence. There's nothing but pure existence. Peace.

Calm. Serenity.

Now, again intentionally go to one of the rooms with thoughts. Choose the worst one, with the loudest worries, most negative thoughts, problems that bother you the most.

Step in again. Notice the noise. Observe those thoughts. Watch them from the side, without engaging.

You feel differently now because you know now that you can leave whenever you want.

Now, go again to your safe room, a white and quiet room. Open that door again and feel the silence and peace. Get there. There are no thoughts, just absolute peace.

Now you know that there are a few rooms in your mind. But there's always one safe room, where you can enter and rest. Be there whenever you feel you want to rest from your thoughts. And, if sometimes you find yourself in loud, negative thinking, don't fight, don't blame yourself, just be aware you have entered a room with thoughts. Remind yourself that you can always exit that loud room and get back to your white and peaceful room.

Now, stay in that room. Watch around. This is the first time you realize that you can see the peace and hear the silence. Acknowledge there is a space in your room without thoughts. You have the power to choose to be there whenever you want.

# Guided Mindfulness Meditation for Overcoming Anxiety

45 min

Welcome to the guided mindfulness meditation for overcoming anxiety. Being mindful means being consciously present and aware of everything around you and within you.

If you suffer from anxiety, know that you are not alone. It's a pretty common issue these days. Most likely, you feel in danger most of the time, although nothing endangers you. Your mind is doing its best to protect you, turning on the "fight or flight "mode, preparing your body to run or fight. But, since there is no real need for that, this state of mind and body does more harm than good for you.

It will help if you tell your mind, "It's okay; we are safe; you don't need to protect me so hard."

This meditation will help you to tell it the way your mind understands. When you manage o calm down your breathing and body, you'll turn off the "fight or flight "button, and eventually, your mind will be assured everything's fine and give up from overprotecting you.

Anxiety is often caused by constant racing of our minds. You should know that you are not alone in this—many people all around the world search for ways to cope with anxiety. Mindfulness can tremendously help here. Since anxiety is a consequence of being mentally too much in the future, bringing awareness to the present can make a world of difference. Being mindful means finding that golden point of awareness and being completely present.

By choosing to take time to meditate and learn how to be more mindful, you have already made the first step towards overcoming anxiety.

During this meditation, we'll calm and slow your breathing, focus on physical sensations, relax the whole body, and be consciously present for a while. Focusing on physical sensations will ground you and help you getting out of your head and calming your busy mind while relaxation will help you get out of fight or flight mode.

I invite you to find some quiet place and make yourself comfortable. Experiencing ease in your body will help you feel the same for your mind. You can sit on a floor, on a chair, or lye, whichever you like. Make sure that your clothes are comfortable, that all tight pieces of clothes or belts are loosened, and you are not too warm or too cold. If you want to practice this meditation before sleep, get ready for bed as you usually do.

Focus on my voice. I will guide you through this experience. We'll try to achieve complete awareness and presence. I suggest you do this meditation with your eyes gently open. You can close them later during the meditation, but try to stay alert.

Focus your vision on a particular point in front of you. Narrow your focus on that point and allow everything else to fade away into the background.

Now, slowly broaden your field of view and allow the background to come into your eye vision. With awareness, notice everything you can see. Don't turn your head; just look consciously at everything in your view. What colors can you see? Try not to name them or judge if you like them or not. Just notice the colors, their shades, the textures, materials. Notice all the tiny details you wouldn't notice otherwise.

Our breathing is so simple yet the most powerful way to ground ourselves in the present.

Bring attention to your breathing. Notice the natural depth and rhythm of your breathing. Don't try to change it, for now, just notice. Listen to the sound of your breathing. Now, look for any movement in your body connected to breathing.

Now, intentionally begin to deepen your inhale and slow down your exhale.

Breathe in through your nose, counting to four. One, two, three, four.

Then breathe out, also through the nose, counting to six. One, two, three, four, five, six.

Repeat it a few times. Inhale. One, two, three, four.
Exhale – one, two, three, four, five, six.
Breathing that way, with exhales longer than inhales, will relax you and tell your mind everything's okay. You are safe. You don't need to run away nor to fight. You can rest and relax.
Take time to notice all there is to experience about your breath.
Focus on those still moments, pauses between every two breaths. Feel the air filling your body and leaving it. Feel its way, from your nostrils, all the way to your lungs, and back outside.
Once again, breathe in – one, two, three, four. And breathe out – one, two, three, four, five, six.
If your regular breathing is too shallow or deeper than that, or can't reach those numbers, don't force it. Just try to breathe out a bit longer than you breathe in.
There are certainly some thoughts going through your mind. Don't stress yourself about it. Your mind is used to be busy. Just let them pass. Imagine your thoughts and worries as colorful balloons flying away. As your breathing is slowing down, your mind is slowing down, too. There are fewer balloons there, and they fly slower and slower.
With special attention, notice pauses between each breath and a similar pause between your thoughts. Mentally link those two. Allow yourself to be in this gap between every two breaths and thoughts. Allow your attention to rest in this space. If your thoughts are still wandering, and you tend to follow them, come back to your breath and the gap between breaths.
Now, broaden your awareness of physical experience.
Bring attention to your body. Feel the points of touch with the surface below you. You might feel the line of connection blurred, or you might experience it as warmth or pressure. Feel your feet on the surface, or your back on the surface of the chair. If you are lying, feel the all touching surface – your back, the backside of your legs and arms, the back of your head. Feel the texture of the surface, its temperature. Is it a cold, smooth floor, or a soft bed covers, your favorite chair, or a cushion you're sitting on, feel it.
Be aware of any sense that you can smell. Focus on scents you can feel.
Then bring your attention to sounds. What can you hear? Perhaps you can listen to some sounds from the outside – traffic, birds, voices. Or some constant sounds of appliances in the home. Hear the sound of your breathing. Acknowledge the rhythm of your heartbeat. Notice the details in the sounds you are hearing. There are always many sounds around us; it's just a matter of focus if we will acknowledge them.
Bring your attention to the surface of your body, your skin. Be aware of everything that touches your skin. Feel the brush of your clothes, the touch of your bed shits, or covers if you are lying.
Feel the temperature of the space you are in.
Take a deep breath, filling your stomach. Exhale as slowly as you can.
Spend some time simply being. Be aware of everything within you and around you. Feel the beat of your heart and the flow of your blood within you.
Bring awareness to your body. Try to feel the aliveness in all the parts of it. Nothing can ground you at this moment better than awareness of sensations in your body.
Take a deep breath, taking the air deeply, so your stomach expands like a balloon.
Breathin out, focus on your hands, fingers, and palms. Feel aliveness in those areas. Simply be aware of all the sensations in this part. You may feel it as warmth or tingling. If you feel the urge to move your fingers or hands, allow yourself to do it. Feel the movement, be aware of every sensation.
Bring awareness to your arms. Notice everything you can feel on and within them, from wrists to your shoulders. Feel the touch with the surface on the backside. Feel the temperature of the air around on your skin. Being so aware of a particular body part means you are already relaxing that part.
Bring awareness to your toes and feet. Feel the tingling in your toes, the relaxed feeling in your feet. Then allow this relaxed feeling to spread up to your ankles, your inner legs, your knees, and upper legs. Focus on all the sensations in your whole legs – warmth, the point of touch between the surface and your skin. Acknowledge the sense of relaxation in your hips, glutes, and pelvic area.

Then continue, moving your awareness up, to your stomach and chest. Be aware of your stomach moving up and down in the rhythm of your breathing. Feel the air expanding your stomach and chest, and leaving it with the exhale.

Breathe in, to the count of four. One, two, three, four. Breathe out, to the count of six. One, two, three, four, five, six.

Repeat it a few times, focusing your undivided attention to the way of the air in through your nose, to the lungs, and your stomach, and all the way back.

Put special attention on still periods between every two segments of breathing. Feel grounded, and allow yourself to sink deeper into the surface.

If any thought arises, just imagine it like a colorful balloon and let it fly by. Resist the impulse to follow it. Just stay outside of it and observe it. You are not your thoughts. Your thoughts have no power over you. Acknowledge they're just that – thoughts, products of your mind.

Continue gradually moving this relaxed scan of your body. Bring awareness to your back. Feel the surface above it. Focus on sensations in your back muscles. Scan them by your awareness, one by one, starting from the lowest point. Feel the heaviness and warmth in your back muscles and your spine. If you can feel any tension remain in your back, give some special attention to that point until you feel it melting and releasing.

Bring awareness to your neck. Feel the weight of the head it holds. Acknowledge all the sensations in your throat.

Bring awareness to the crown of your head. How often are you aware of it? It's time to give it your attention. If you have hair, feel the touch of it on your head. Take a breath in and imagine you are inhaling pure peace. Allow it to spread through your head, relaxing all the muscles.

Focus on each muscle on your face, one by one. Scan them with your awareness. Become aware of any sensation in your eyes and your mouth. You can close your eyes if you want.

Take a few deep breaths again. With each inhale, imagine you are breathing in peace, tranquility, and relaxation. With exhale, let go of everything that doesn't serve your peace of mind and body. Imagine you are breathing out all the tension, and feel your body getting softer, heavier, and relaxed. Let it sink into the surface beneath you, completely supported.

Feel the temperature of the air around you. Feel it with your palms, your lips, your forehead, your lower legs.

What can you hear now? Try to count all the sounds you can listen to at the moment. Focus on each of them for a while. Imagine them entering your ears.

If there is any area of your body that is not relaxed yet, give it special attention. It is trying to tell you something. Sometimes, giving special attention to some sensation in our body is enough to make it soften and fade away. Bring your attention to the areas of your body that are telling you something. Notice the sensation and stay with it for some time. If your mind is drifting to overthinking or old patterns of thinking, gently come back and stay with the experience of the sensation.

Take a deep breath. Exhale slowly. Each inhale is bringing you peace and healing.

Every exhale takes away everything you need to let go of.

Every moment is so beneficial for you.

Imagine what's going on within your body now – your organs, your muscles, your bones, your nervous system – all of that is feeling your peace and are relaxing. Now you are giving them time to heal and recharge. This is healing for you.

Inhale peace. Exhale anxiety.

Inhale tranquility. Exhale tension.

Inhale calmness. Exhale rush.

You are present and aware now. This is how it looks like to be mindful. This moment is the only reality that exists for you. There's no such thing as the past or the future. If you have any worries lingering in some corner of the mind, imagine it as a balloon you're holding. Open your hand and let it fly away. If you still have more worries bothering you, imagine you are holding a bunch of balloons. Let them all fly into the sky. You are the only one who is holding them here. You don't need them anymore. Worries are just a way your mind is playing tricks on you. You don't have to follow them nor to engage. Whenever you notice that you are about to lose yourself in your thoughts, bring your attention back to your breathing, surrounding, and your physical sensations.

When you are completely aware, grounded in the present, anxiety can't survive. It must fly away with all the colorful balloons you are letting go of.

Take another full breath again. Fill your stomach and your chest with peace and calmness. Breathe out as slowly as you can, letting go of each and every remaining piece of anxiety, tension, and busy mind.

You can start over with your aware presence as many times as you need.

In your usual life outside the meditation, look for patterns and situations when you might be rushing. Then intentionally slow down and come back to experience life fully. When we try to control life, and we constantly rush, we can't experience it fully. On the contrary, when we slow down and stay with our sensations, we can notice more, experience more, live more fully, and savor life. So, allow yourself to slow down and rest in the gap between thoughts. When you quiet the noise in your head, you are able to see, hear, and feel everything around you, you are aware and open to life.

When you feel ready, gently open your eyes, stretch yourself, get up, and move on with your daily activities.

# Affirmations for overcoming anxiety

60 min

Listen to these affirmations and repeat them mentally or out loud:
I'm aware of my breathing. I'm aware of the air going in and out of my body.
I'm aware of my body. I'm aware of my heart rhythm.
I'm aware of my fears and anxiety. I'm aware of the discomfort I feel.
I'm aware of the negative thoughts that make me feel anxious.
Now, I'm slowly calming my mind.
I'm calming my anxiety.
I'm relaxing my body and slowing down my thoughts.
I'm letting go of negative thoughts.
I'm letting go of fears and concerns.
Each moment, I'm finding more peace.
I am safe.
Being aware of my breathing, I'm letting go of everything I don't need anymore.
I inhale serenity.
Everything is just the way it should be.
Everything's happening for my higher good.
I am divinely protected and guided.
Everything happens when the time is right.
Whatever I need comes to me.
Whatever I should know, reveals to me.
I am calm and relaxed.
I am in peace with the world.
I am in peace with life.
The world is a safe place for me.
I am powerful.
I am strong.
I am present and grounded.
I am in perfect balance.
I inhale calmness. I exhale peace.
While breathing, smile at yourself.
I am safe and secure. I give myself permission to be in peace.
I'm well.
Things are getting better and better every day.
I expect great things to happen.
I accept my anxiety. It's just trying to protect me. Thank you. But, I don't need you anymore. I am safe now, and I am letting you go.
Feel the lightness.
I accept all of my emotions and allow myself to experience them.
They don't define me. I can watch them while remaining calm.
I'm healing all the time.
My body and mind are in a healthy harmony.
I allow myself to be in peace.

I feel born again.
I feel wellness in the whole body, in each cell of my body.
I am full of energy.
I allow myself to rest in this comfort and peace.
I enjoy this tranquility and gentleness.
I enjoy being in this completely relaxed state, free from anxiety.
I'm aware of my breathing. I'm aware of the air going in and out of my body.
I'm aware of my body. I'm aware of my heart rhythm.
I'm aware of my fears and anxiety. I'm aware of the discomfort I feel.
I'm aware of the negative thoughts that make me feel anxious.
Now, I'm slowly calming my mind.
I'm calming my anxiety.
I'm relaxing my body and slowing down my thoughts.
I'm letting go of negative thoughts.
I'm letting go of fears and concerns.
Each moment, I'm finding more peace.
I am safe.
Being aware of my breathing, I'm letting go of everything I don't need anymore.
I inhale serenity.
Everything is just the way it should be.
Everything's happening for my higher good.
I am divinely protected and guided.
Everything happens when the time is right.
Whatever I need comes to me.
Whatever I should know, reveals to me.
I am calm and relaxed.
I am in peace with the world.
I am in peace with life.
The world is a safe place for me.
I am powerful.
I am strong.
I am present and grounded.
I am in perfect balance.
I inhale calmness. I exhale peace.
While breathing, smile at yourself.
I am safe and secure. I give myself permission to be in peace.
I'm well.
Things are getting better and better every day.
I expect great things to happen.
I accept my anxiety. It's just trying to protect me. Thank you. But, I don't need you anymore. I am safe now, and I am letting you go.
Feel the lightness.
I accept all of my emotions and allow myself to experience them.
They don't define me. I can watch them while remaining calm.
I'm healing all the time.
My body and mind are in a healthy harmony.
I allow myself to be in peace.
I feel born again.
I feel wellness in the whole body, in each cell of my body.

I am full of energy.
I allow myself to rest in this comfort and peace.
I enjoy this tranquility and gentleness.
I enjoy being in this completely relaxed state, free from anxiety.
I'm aware of my breathing. I'm aware of the air going in and out of my body.
I'm aware of my body. I'm aware of my heart rhythm.
I'm aware of my fears and anxiety. I'm aware of the discomfort I feel.
I'm aware of the negative thoughts that make me feel anxious.
Now, I'm slowly calming my mind.
I'm calming my anxiety.
I'm relaxing my body and slowing down my thoughts.
I'm letting go of negative thoughts.
I'm letting go of fears and concerns.
Each moment, I'm finding more peace.
I am safe.
Being aware of my breathing, I'm letting go of everything I don't need anymore.
I inhale serenity.
Everything is just the way it should be.
Everything's happening for my higher good.
I am divinely protected and guided.
Everything happens when the time is right.
Whatever I need comes to me.
Whatever I should know, reveals to me.
I am calm and relaxed.
I am in peace with the world.
I am in peace with life.
The world is a safe place for me.
I am powerful.
I am strong.
I am present and grounded.
I am in perfect balance.
I inhale calmness. I exhale peace.
While breathing, smile at yourself.
I am safe and secure. I give myself permission to be in peace.
I'm well.
Things are getting better and better every day.
I expect great things to happen.
I accept my anxiety. It's just trying to protect me. Thank you. But, I don't need you anymore. I am safe now, and I am letting you go.
Feel the lightness.
I accept all of my emotions and allow myself to experience them.
They don't define me. I can watch them while remaining calm.
I'm healing all the time.
My body and mind are in a healthy harmony.
I allow myself to be in peace.
I feel born again.
I feel wellness in the whole body, in each cell of my body.
I am full of energy.
I allow myself to rest in this comfort and peace.

I enjoy this tranquility and gentleness.
I enjoy being in this completely relaxed state, free from anxiety.
I'm aware of my breathing. I'm aware of the air going in and out of my body.
I'm aware of my body. I'm aware of my heart rhythm.
I'm aware of my fears and anxiety. I'm aware of the discomfort I feel.
I'm aware of the negative thoughts that make me feel anxious.
Now, I'm slowly calming my mind.
I'm calming my anxiety.
I'm relaxing my body and slowing down my thoughts.
I'm letting go of negative thoughts.
I'm letting go of fears and concerns.
Each moment, I'm finding more peace.
I am safe.
Being aware of my breathing, I'm letting go of everything I don't need anymore.
I inhale serenity.
Everything is just the way it should be.
Everything's happening for my higher good.
I am divinely protected and guided.
Everything happens when the time is right.
Whatever I need comes to me.
Whatever I should know, reveals to me.
I am calm and relaxed.
I am in peace with the world.
I am in peace with life.
The world is a safe place for me.
I am powerful.
I am strong.
I am present and grounded.
I am in perfect balance.
I inhale calmness. I exhale peace.
While breathing, smile at yourself .
I am safe and secure. I give myself permission to be in peace.
I'm well.
Things are getting better and better every day.
I expect great things to happen.
I accept my anxiety. It's just trying to protect me.Thank you. But, I don't need you anymore. I am safe now, and I am letting you go.
Feel the lightness.
I accept all of my emotions and allow myself to experience them.
They don't define me. I can watch them while remaining calm.
I'm healing all the time.
My body and mind are in a healthy harmony.
I allow myself to be in peace.
I feel born again.
I feel wellness in the whole body, in each cell of my body.
I am full of energy.
I allow myself to rest in this comfort and peace.
I enjoy this tranquility and gentleness.
I enjoy being in this completely relaxed state, free from anxiety.

# Guided Meditation For Overcoming Depression

40 min

Welcome to the meditation created to help you with depression. You can use it to overcome depressive moods, too.
It's going to bring you a new perspective and show you a new way to look at your thoughts and feelings. You might feel better as soon as you finish the meditation session. You'll feel more hopeful immediately. If you regularly practice this meditation, depressed moods will occur less often until you finally notice depression has entirely disappeared from your life.
Please, keep in mind that this meditation is aimed to ease depression and help you during the process, but it can't replace professional help. Please, seek professional help, and use this meditation in addition.
Choose a time when you won't be disturbed, and you can safely close your eyes, listen, and relax for a while. This quiet, me-time is not a luxury. It's a need and will tremendously add to your healing.
Before we begin, take time to find a comfortable position. You can be lying or sitting up. It's up to you, and everything is okay as long as your back is straight and has its natural curve.
Make sure that your clothes are comfortable, loosen all the restrictive pieces or belts. Turn off any ringers and notifications.
Place hands beside the body, or on your lap, or knees, palms up.
If you wish, close your eyes. If you don't feel so, it's okay, too.
Take a few deep and slow breaths. Connect with your breath. Observe how it affects your body, notice all the sensations and movements connected with it. Feel the air entering your nostrils. Notice your belly rises and falls with the in-breath and out-breath.
Now allow your breathing to settle in its natural rhythm and let go of trying to control it.
Be aware of your body, posture, its place in the space, and its weight on the surface beneath.
Notice all the sensations in the body. Feel all the body parts.
Be aware of your breathing and its natural rhythm.
Depression is universal; it's part of being a human. We all feel depressed from time to time. But when it lasts for a long time, it affects everything - our body and health, our mindset and thinking, emotions, and life fields. There's a whole package of negative feelings coming from depression. It can make you look at life through black glasses and being unable to see anything positive. Eventually, it seems as if all of your interests have faded away.
Depression is a natural reaction to loss. However, you can be depressed for no apparent reason, too. That doesn't make your depression any easier, nor it means anything's wrong with you. Either way, know that your thoughts and emotions are normal.
Although it's tough and not fun at all, depression can bring you something good, too - It can force you to turn inward, examine your problems and perspectives, gain meaningful insights, reevaluate things in your life and make adjustments.
Living with depression for sure is not something you should accept as permanent. Know that there is always a solution out there. Seek professional help, support from people around you, and use this meditation as often as you can. This meditation will teach you some techniques that will help you a lot to feel better. You can use them whenever you need them.
Whatever your emotions and thoughts are, you should not ignore, suppress, nor deny them. Whatever you fight or deny, grows stronger. The solution is also not in digging for the root of the problems and figuring out where they came from. Those are not the ways to get rid of negative thoughts and feelings. A better solution is to change your relationship with them. Instead of resisting and fighting hard feelings, accept

them, make space for them to play, and stay with them for a while. Give them your attention; your emotions are trying to tell you something. They are telling you where you were not faithful to your true self.

When you offer them acceptance instead of resistance, you'll see, much to your surprise, how they lose the power and fade away.

Make yourself comfortable so that you can relax. If you fall asleep during the meditation, it's okay; your subconscious mind will be listening to and recording everything I say. But, if possible, try to stay alert during the session, so you can consciously engage in healing.

Breathe in your natural pattern. You don't need to change your rhythm nor depth of breathing for now. Just breathe in your usual way. Place your attention on the nose. Feel the air entering your nostrils. Feel its coolness. Now, notice the air leaving your nostrils, notice its warmth. Do this for a few moments. Focus on breathing the fresh air in and breathing warm air out. Concentrate only on sensations in your nose.

Do it once again—cool air in, warm air out.

Now, explore your breath and allow yourself to experience it fully. Watch your breath, be curious. Have the experience of breathing and observe yourself having it at the same time.

If your natural breathing is long and deep, notice that. If your normal breathing is short and shallow, notice that, too, without judgment. If the way your breathing changes or stays the same, notice that. Don't try to change or fix anything. Don't hold for beliefs of "how things should be." Instead, accept the things for what they are and just observe without trying to control them.

So, we are still observing your natural breathing pattern.

Sooner or later, you will lose your focus. It's perfectly normal, so don't criticize or judge yourself. We all get distracted, and focusing requires some practice.

Distractions always come from one of these sources - your thoughts, senses, or feelings. When a distraction occurs, just notice it and let go. Then gently bring your focus back to your breath. Try to do it for a moment, with the next distraction. Notice, and let go. No need to push it away. Don't fight it, don't suppress it, just let it float by.

Whenever your mind begins to wander, notice what's going on. Bring your attention back to your nose, sensations in it, breathing in and out.

It's also expected to feel the urge to name a distraction. For instance, you may mentally say, "alarm is ringing in the next apartment," "kids are making noise outside," "traffic," "dog's barking," or so, whatever distracted you. Try to name just one thing instead, more general and more in connection with what's happening with you - "distracting" or "wandering," for instance. Bring your attention back to your breathing. Try this for a moment, with the next distraction or mind wandering.

Now, the next time you lose your focus, try not to name things internally at all. Just notice that you have lost your focus and bring it back. Try this with the next distraction.

Most likely, depressive thoughts and feelings will intrude. Those are ones you are trying to escape from. The trick is to learn to bring your attention back to your breathing instead of following those thoughts. Breathe in your natural way. When a negative thought arises, just notice it and let it pass by. It will be easier each time because you already know how to let thoughts go. Gently bring your focus back to your nose and your breathing. Try it for a moment. Notice the negative thought occurring. Let it float by you, easily, without pushing.

When you feel depressed, your mind is often stuck in the past, ruminating about some things from the past that affected your life. Being in the present, consciously aware, makes you balanced. You are the most present when focusing on your breath and sensations in your body. That makes you grounded in the present.

Try to be consciously present and aware of each moment of your next few breaths. Feel the air entering your nostrils. Feel its coolness. Feel it as it goes down your airways to your lungs and belly. Notice all the movements connected with breath. Feel all the sensation it provokes in your body. Follow its way back, and feel the warmth of the air leaving your nostrils.

Doing this, be intentionally present and completely aware of every moment of your next few breaths.

Don't be surprised when negative emotions occur and distract you. They go hand in hand with depressive thoughts. You'll probably experience sadness, emptiness, anxiety, resentment, bitterness, anger, or rage. Emotions are nothing else but a combination of your thoughts and sensations in your body. Acknowledge that and mentally divide a negative emotion into those two parts. Notice the thought in your mind and feel the sense it provokes in your body. You might feel it as tension in your head or neck, a weight on your chest, fatigue, monotony, or an ache in different body parts. Allow yourself to experience what you feel. You don't need to change it, solve it, or take any action about it.

The second part is to see the thoughts in your mind. Acknowledge the connection between those two. Your thoughts provoke your body to feel a certain way, and you experience those two together as an emotion.

Make a conscious choice to place your attention on the sensation in your body, not the thought. Rest your attention on the sensation. Notice if its intensity changes or stays the same. It might happen to disappear under your focused attention.

Now, leave the emotion and the sensation in the body and gently bring your attention back to the breathing and the way it feels in your nose. Breathe in and feel the cool air entering your nose. Breathe out, and focus on the warmth of the air that's leaving your nose.

If you choose to follow your distressing thoughts, it will strengthen the connected negative feeling. But, if you choose to pay undivided attention to the negative sensations, it provokes in your body, depressive and distressing thoughts diminish. They need your negative thoughts and their stories to feed themselves. If you focus only on your physical sensations, negative emotions starve and fade away, bringing you relief.

Notice that focusing on your breathing and physical sensation grounds you in the present and brings you relief better than anything else.

Now, visualize you are at a train station. People are rushing in all directions. There are the hustle and bustle all around you. You are standing still on your platform, waiting for your train. The world around you seems dull and grey—colorless people in their grey suits, dirty streets around the station, grey station, and ugly trains. You are wearing a plain, grey pelerine with no defined shape. You are also carrying a heavy bag made of dark leather. It's so heavy that your arms sore. But you can't put it down. You have to carry it wherever you go.

Thoughts may come and go in their rhythm while you are observing the world around you. Don't worry- all the mental chatter will pass; just let the thoughts be and be gentle with yourself. People and your thoughts are passing you by in their busy manner, but you remain completely calm. You know you will be leaving this hectic environment in a moment, as soon as your train arrives. Think of this moment as an escape that will help you think clearly again. The train will take you to a far destination, where you feel peaceful and calm. You know you'll come back as a different person. You are ready to begin the journey. Your train arrives, and you are stepping abroad. Give yourself permission to devote this time to yourself, to spend some time alone, to relax. You know you'll gain a new perspective, and you also know that this has to be done. So, don't feel guilty. You find your carriage. It's empty, and you are the only passenger here. Take a seat and finally put your heavy beg down. It's such a relief! Your muscles automatically relax. The sense of tranquility fills your mind and body.

The voices from the station start to fade away. You are looking through a window. That's the same dull and grey world out there, but you can observe it from a distance now. You are leaving it behind now, and it's natural to feel sadness and regret, or relief, knowing that you are leaving everything that was holding you back.

Take this me-time to rest and relax. Allow yourself to see your needs and desires. Your sadness is trying to tell you something. Perhaps it's trying to show you that you have neglected your needs and needs of your soul. It suffers and uses unpleasant feelings to gain your attention. You have enough time to relax the whole body.

You've created a distance now, and you can see your life from another perspective. From your window, the world outside looks different now. The sky looks more blue and clear, the grass and trees are greener. The further you get from the train station, the easier you feel. Your feel calm and positive. Your arms and hands are rested from heavy baggage. Your muscles are relaxed in a comfortable seat. Your breathing is deep and slow. Your stomach is quiet and steady. Your legs and feet are comfortable and relaxed. Your mind slows down to a pleasant speed. You feel free to just be yourself, in balance, and let everything just be as it is.

As it reaches your destination, the train stops. You pick up your heavy, black bag and step off the train. You have just a few more streets to walk to your special place.

The bag is too heavy, but you know it will be over soon. You feel stronger now, determined, and enthusiastic.

Here you are, in front of a large gate. You open it with effort. You are in your private garden. It's been a long time since you were here last time. It looks neglected. No one was taking care of it while you were occupied with your sadness and pain. You step on the path that leads through the garden. There are no flowers, nor grass. Where there were weeds, there are no flowers. You go to an old tree on the backside of the garden. There's a spade recumbent to the tree. You are taking it and starting to dig. You are digging a hole in the shade of the tree. Once the digging is done, you open the bag, curious to find out what was the heavy baggage you carried around. To your surprise, the bag is full of your worries, your fears, sadness, anger, and regrets. You can see them as large, heavy stones. It's time to bury them. Visualize you are taking the rocks, one by one, and drop them in the hole. Name your stones by your hard feelings and mentally say to each of them while laying it into the ground, "I'm letting you go."

Let go of sadness.
Let go of regrets.
Let go of anger.
Let go of self-doubt.
Let go of resentment.
Let go of bitterness.
Let go of monotony.
Let go of hatred.
Let go of jealousy.
Let go of misery.
Let go of helplessness.
Let go of hopelessness.
Let go of fears.
Let go of the pain.
Let go of suffering.
Let go of everything that makes you feel bad.
Let go of sadness.
Let go of regrets.
Let go of anger.
Let go of self-doubt.
Let go of resentment.
Let go of bitterness.
Let go of monotony.
Let go of hatred.
Let go of jealousy.
Let go of misery.

Let go of helplessness.
Let go of hopelessness.
Let go of fears.
Let go of the pain.
Let go of suffering.
Let go of everything that makes you feel bad.

Do this as long as you need to bury all of the stones from your bag. In the end, bury the bag, too. Bury the hole and feel the relief.
Go back to an old bench in the middle of the garden. Take a seat and enjoy the feeling of ease and freedom. Feel the lightness. Notice the sun is shining through the trees. Look around. Nurturing this garden will need just a little energy to fix everything and bring its old glow. Taking care of this place is the priority now. You'll enjoy every moment of it and the results.
Rest deeply in your garden, imaging its final look when you take care of everything. Inhale the sunlight. Exhale peace. Look at colorful flowers. Smell the roses. Feel the enthusiasm. Realize that your journey brought you here to remind you of who you really are. Your old self is back. Smile to who you really are. Enjoy watching the dance of light and shadows in your garden, and mentally say to yourself:
I am free.
I am relaxed.
I am peaceful.
I am grateful.
I am light.
I am happy.
I am energetic.
I am full of love.
I am calm.
I am safe.
I am powerful.
I am joyful.
Life is good.
Life is colorful.
Life is magnificent.
I love myself.
I know my value.
I appreciate myself.
I accept myself.
I love life.
I am free.
I am relaxed.
I am peaceful.
I am grateful.
I am light.
I am happy.
I am energetic.
I am full of love.
I am calm.
I am safe.
I am powerful.
I am joyful.

Life is good.
Life is colorful.
Life is magnificent.
I love myself.
I know my value.
I appreciate myself.
I accept myself.
I love life.
I am free.
I am relaxed.
I am peaceful.
I am grateful.
I am light.
I am happy.
I am energetic.
I am full of love.
I am calm.
I am safe.
I am powerful.
I am joyful.
Life is good.
Life is colorful.
Life is magnificent.
I love myself.
I know my value.
I appreciate myself.
I accept myself.
I love life.
I am free.
I am relaxed.
I am peaceful.
I am grateful.
I am light.
I am happy.
I am energetic.
I am full of love.
I am calm.
I am safe.
I am powerful.
I am joyful.
Life is good.
Life is colorful.
Life is magnificent.
I love myself.
I know my value.
I appreciate myself.
I accept myself.
I love life.

Breathe deeply and smile to yourself with every exhale.

Enjoy for a while in this relaxed state, feeling warm sunlight on your skin. You can take this feeling with you.

When you come back from this trip to your usual daily life, you will have a completely different perspective.

Your private garden will always be there for you, and you can come back whenever you wish.

When you feel ready, gently open your eyes and go on with your usual daily activities. Or, you can drift off to sleep and have a relaxing, deep rest.

# Guided Meditation For Overcoming Insomnia

35 min

Good evening. Welcome to the guided meditation, which is aimed to help you overcome insomnia. If you have problems with falling asleep or staying asleep during the night, this meditation is for you. You can use it whether you often have trouble sleeping or just from time to time. It's not pleasant at all to lie sleepless and feel exhausted the next day, unable to afford a quality rest to your body and mind.

Use this meditation before sleep as a part of your evening routine. Prepare yourself for bed in your usual way, lie, and find the most comfortable position. The temperature should also be pleasant, not too warm, nor cold. You can lie on your back or on the side, whatever best helps you to relax. I invite you to listen to my voice. It will guide you, help you relax, and take you to a calm, calm state from which you can easily fall asleep.

Words in this meditation will talk to your conscious and subconscious mind. That way, it will help you easily fall asleep and stay asleep for the whole night. Finally, you'll have a recharging, restful sleep. The first time since long ago, you won't wake up during the night, and you'll finally feel rested and refreshed in the morning.

This might not happen the first few times you do this meditation. What will undoubtedly happen is that you will relax more and be feel less tensed. Good night's sleep is a habit. To build a habit of easily falling asleep and staying asleep during the night, you will need some time and practice. But it's established, it will pay off in levels of energy and life satisfaction. So it's worth a try. We recommend you be patient and consistent in using this meditation every night before sleep. It will undoubtedly lead to forming better sleep habits and eventually overcoming insomnia.

The first time you fall asleep in moments and stay asleep until the morning comes, wake up renewed and fresh, you'll realize that all the efforts have paid off, and this was the best thing you could do for yourself. We often have hard times trying to relax and fall asleep because our minds refuse to calm and stop thinking. When our bodies calm down to rest, our brain seems to find it the best time to go into overdrive. If you are one of the people who overthink, especially when it's time for sleep, you can't stop mentally repeating, and it would be best to write it all down. That way, you'll put it aside for later, without worry that you might forget something important, and you'll free up space in your mind, allowing it to calm down. So, pause the meditation and download it all from your mind to the paper. Your actions and concerns can wait. Now it is time for rest.

I invite you to put your attention to my voice and ground yourself in this very moment. Feel the comfort and the warmth of your bed. Feel the ease because it is a time when you don't need to do anything. This is time only for you and your reenergizing. You don't have to do a thing. Just listen to my voice without any expectation nor insisting on falling asleep. Even if you stay awake all night long, this meditation will bring you relaxation and rest. So don't put any pressure on yourself. All you need to do is lying in your bed, listening to the words, and relaxing. If sleep comes, great. If not, not a big deal, it's okay, too. You will rest anyway.

Take a deep breath in, to the count of four. Hold the breath to the count of three. Breathe out as slowly as you can, counting to six.

Repeat it a few more times. Take a deep breath in, to the count of four. Hold the breath to the count of three. Breathe out, as slowly as you can, counting to six.

Do it once again - take a breath, one, two, three, four. Hold it, one, two, three. Exhale, one, two, three, four, five, six.

And, one more time - breathe in deeply, counting to four. Hold breath the count of three. Then, breathe out, counting to six.

If you can't reach these numbers, it's okay, too. Don't force yourself; do what you can. Then, allow your breathing to fall into its usual rhythm.

With each breath out, allow your body to relax a bit more and sink deeper into the surface.

Now, see your thoughts come and go. They do it all the time. Your busy mind is used to produce them all the time. But you don't have to follow each of them. It may be such a precious insight – you are not your thoughts. Even more, you are always choosing which of them you want to think about. They are just products of your mind, and you are the one who decides. So, if you're going to rest your busy mind and fall asleep, let your thoughts float by, like little clouds or soap bubbles. Since you can't forbid your mind to do its job and create thoughts, the only thing you can do is to remove your focus from them. Focus on something else, and unwanted thoughts will lose their power and diminish. Eventually, your mind will slow down and stop creating them. That's why mindful focus on your breathing, physical sensations, and environment can go a long way to relax and calm a busy mind.

First, bring your awareness to your body and its sensations. That is the first step towards mindful presence. Notice how your body feels. Acknowledge its posture, feel the temperature of your body and space around. Feel the support of the surface below you and the comfort of your mattress. Feel the weight of your body and the weights of bed covers. Feel your heartbeat and notice the rhythm of your blood flow. Focus on your breathing and listen to its sound. Place your attention on your nose. Feel the air entering your nostrils and going down to fill your lungs. Fill the stomach with the air and allow it to inflate like a balloon. Then follow the way of the breath back, notice how it leaves your stomach, your lungs, and finally, your nostrils. Notice the coolness of the air you are inhaling and the warmth of it on the exhale when it went throughout your body.

Focus only on your breathing and movement and sensations it provokes in your body. It is the easiest and quickest way to ground yourself and relax.

How do your feet feel? How do your legs feel? Notice sensations in each part of the body. How your glutes and the pelvic area feel? What do you feel in your stomach? How does your back feel? Notice all the sensations in your fingers, hands, and arms. Acknowledge how your shoulders and neck feel. Then bring your awareness to sensations in your head and face. If there is any tension in your body, acknowledge it. Allow all the tension to arise from all the deep or hidden corners of your body, coming up to the surface. When you feel that all the tension is collected on your skin, let it go.

Take a deep breath, and with exhale, let go of tension.

Repeat this a few times until you feel your body is completely relaxed, free from any tension.

Do a quick scan of the whole body, part by part, checking if all the parts are relaxed.

If you find any tension, simply let it go with breathing out.

There are so many things you can place your focus on right now. Even the busiest mind calms when you are mindful and truly present.

Sooner or later, your focus will drift off from your breathing and physical sensations. Gently bring them back. Concentrating on the feelings in your body and your breathing is the simplest yet most powerful way to stay present and grounded, calm, and relax.

Thoughts will eventually appear in your mind. Don't stress about it. Notice them, and let go. Do it as many times as needed, always bringing your focus back to your breath and your body. Notice the air entering your nose, and stay with the breath throughout the body, moment by moment. That is a natural way to calm and, after some time, drift off to sleep.

Breathe in, breathe out, and with a smile, greet the feeling of relaxation and letting go. This is time only for you. This is time to recharge and gaining fresh energy. Stretch your body and feel how comfortable it is to lie in your bed, having nothing else to do. The night is meant for having rest from everyone and everything, even our thoughts. With every breath, dive deeper into the sense of comfort and relaxation.

Visualize, you are in a kanu boat, on calm, clear water. The boat is floating in the place, cradling you gently. Listen to the sounds of water. Your eyes are closed, the sun is shining tenderly on your skin. Your boat is incredibly comfortable, soft like a cloud, yet strong enough to support you. You are safe and calm. Feel the joy and the ease of the moment. It's beautiful. Breathe in, breathe out, and smile to yourself.

The boat is large enough for your whole body to lie comfortably. It's time for you to relax the whole body, part by part, by scanning it with your mindful attention, healing light, and your inner smile. Relax your toes and feet. Allow them gently open to the ceiling. Relax all the muscles of your legs. Relax your lower and upper legs and knees. Relax your hips and pelvic area. Relax your glutes and notice how the whole lower part of the body is relaxed. Allow your fingers to relax, and your palms opened up to the ceiling. Relax your wrists and whole hands and arms.

Place your inner smile into your belly. Feel the calmness and peace in your stomach. Allow it to move easily in the rhythm of your breathing. Notice how relaxed it is. Relax your chest, and feel them floating. Now, relax your back, from the lowest point, up to your neck. Relax your vertebras, one by one, and feel each muscle loose and relax, becoming soft, like during a massage. Breathe in, and breathe out, visualizing you are exhaling through your spine everything you want to let go.

Our shoulders are the most crucial point in relaxation. That's where we hold and carry most of the weight, all our worries, fears, and hard feelings. Most of us go through life not noticing our shoulders are tensed and tight. Relax your shoulders now. Let go of all the weight and let them drop from the ears.

Relax your neck, allowing it to lose and soften, leaving your head cradled by the soft pillow. Open up your throat and allow all the muscles there to relax.

Our central, the head, is often overwhelmed. Let it relax. Relax your scalp and the forehead. Relax your eyebrows and all the tiny muscles around your eyes. Allow your eyes to rest and sink into the head. They work hard all day long. It's time for them to finally have a proper rest. Relax your cheeks and your lips. Release your jaw and allow the base of your tongue to relax. Relax your ears and intentionally release any tension you might be still feeling anywhere in your head and face.

Once again, do a quick scan of the whole body to check if it is completely relaxed.

Your feet – relaxed. Your legs, knees, upper legs – relaxed. Your hips and pelvis – relaxed—your glutes-relaxed. Your hands – relaxed. Your arms, elbows, and upper arms – relaxed. Your belly – relaxed and calm. Your chest – relaxed. Your back, from the bottom to the top – relaxed. Your shoulders and your neck – relaxed. The top and the back of your head – relaxed. Your face – relaxed. Your eye muscles, your nose, your cheeks, your mouth, your jaw – all relaxed.

Now, when all the parts of the body are relaxed, it's time to pay attention to your skin and allow it to relax, too. It works all the time, protecting your body from the outside world, and it needs rest and reenergizing. Visualize the other organs in your body. Take a moment to appreciate everything they do for you all the time. Smile at them with your inner smile, send them love and light, and allow them to relax. Imagine your body on the inside. Imagine your organs working for you all the time. Mentally send them love and let them relax.

Acknowledge that your emotional part needs rest, too. Emotions are turned on all the time, but you don't need them right now. Give your emotions permission to let go. Forgive everything there is to be forgiven. Let go of all negative feelings. The only thing you need now is inner peace and tranquility. Don't hold andy anger, resentment, nor sadness. Let go of everything that doesn't serve you.

If any thoughts occur, and they certainly do, let them pass you by. You don't need any of them right now. It is not time to think or solve problems, to be productive, nor to achieve anything. It is time to rest your mind. Let it recharge now so you could be productive when the time for that comes.

Visualize you are in a dark, empty room. The only thing you can see is a clock on the wall. The clock hands are moving in the speed of your thoughts. The only thing you should do is counting the movements of the clock hands. You find it harder and harder, because they move slower and slower, while you are becoming more and more sleepy. You notice they become slower and slower until they are barely moving. Your mind is calm and clear now, and you are just a step away from drifting off to sleep.

Observe your body becoming heavier and sleepier. You are in a state of deep relaxation now. Watch your slow and deep breathing, your calm mind, and a relaxed body. There's no urge to change anything. There's only calm, mindful observing and acceptance. You feel the warmth, the coziness, the peace, and deep calmness. Everything's calm, peaceful, and easy. Everything you don't need fades away into the blurry background. Inhale. Exhale. This is how it feels to be relaxed on a deeper level.

You are carefree. All is well. Breathe in, breathe out.

Let go of all of your concerns, all the fears, and worries. Everything will be just fine. Everything happens when the time is perfect. Leave everything to higher intelligence, and trust all will be well.

Enjoy the serenity and carefreeness, giving up of control and allow a dream to come.

This is a moment of perfect balance and harmony.

Notice your deep, calm breathing. Feel comfort and ease, becoming one with the moment, giving up any effort. Your body and mind are enjoying these moments of absolute rest.

You are in a forest, high in the mountains. The sun is shining through the trees. You've been hiking in the hills the whole day long. You feel pretty tired now. But your house is still quite far. So you have to walk about an hour more until you get there. You know that a fire in the fireplace, a cozy blanket, and a warm, comfortable bed are waiting for you.

You're stepping down a steep, narrow path. You feel so tired that you start to count your steps to move attention from your soring feet. You are walking and breathing deeply fresh mountain air, counting your breaths out. Breathe in. Breathe out. One. Breathe in. Breathe out, two. Inhale, exhale, three. Breathe in, breathe out, four. Breathe in, breathe out, five.

Your feet are tired. Your legs are sleepy. Your back needs rest. Your mind is sluggish. Your eyes are struggling to stay open. Your hands already sleep. You are yawning, wishing only one thing – to get to the house soon and sink in the bed. You're going down the steep path. You know you have to get there before the day ends. You can hear birds and insects in the grass, your steps down the path, and the sound of your breathing.

You are still breathing deeply, counting on your exhales. The night is about to come. The forest is preparing for sleep. It becomes harder and harder to walk and to count as you become more and more sleepy. You wish to lie under the tree and just allow yourself to fall asleep.

You are yawning and barely can walk. Fortunately, just a few more steps, and you'll get to the small house where you finally can sleep. The Moon and stars appear in the sky. You finally reached your destination. You're opening the wooden door. Your legs are heavy, and you can barely move. The fire is crackling in the fireplace. You are lying on the cozy bed, placing your head onto a soft, fluffy pillow, wrapping yourself in a warm blanket.

You can feel your legs are already sleeping. Your stomach is sleeping. Your back is sleeping. Your head and face are sleeping. Your whole body is sleeping. It's now time to allow your mind to fall asleep, too.

Mentally repeat those statements:

I am calm.
I am peaceful.
I am tranquil.
I am free.
I am worth everything life has to give me.
I am full of love.
I am healing.
I am recharging.
I am reenergizing.
I am resting.
I am divinely supported and guided.
I am safe.
I am secure.

I feel good.
I feel comfortable.
I feel light.
I feel serene.
Everything's all right.
I'm free to rest now.
I am calm.
I am peaceful.
I am tranquil.
I am free.
I am worth everything life has to give me.
I am full of love.
I am healing.
I am recharging.
I am reenergizing.
I am resting.
I am divinely supported and guided.
I am safe.
I am secure.
I feel good.
I feel comfortable.
I feel light.
I feel serene.
Everything's all right.
I'm free to rest now.

While you are falling asleep, acknowledge that all is well. You'll have a good, quality night's rest. You'll fall asleep now, and stay asleep during the whole night. In the morning, you'll wake up refreshed and renewed.
Feel the serenity. Feel the calmness. Feel the tranquility and deep peace. Allow yourself to sink into a deeper sleep, knowing everything is fine. You are calm. You are safe. You are worthy. You deserve good rest.
Step into the sleeping state where the problems of the day are solved. Good night, and have nice sleep.

# Guided Meditation For Self-healing While Sleeping

55 min

Welcome to the meditation for self-healing. Whether you don't feel very well, or you have a diagnose, suffer from chronic pain, this meditation will help you use the ability of your body to heal itself. During this meditation, you'll be talked down into a relaxed state. From that place, you can talk to your body, send love to it, and empower it to heal.

This meditation is aimed to empower the self-healing abilities of your body while you are asleep. If you fall asleep during the meditation, your subconscious mind will listen to my words and help your body in self-healing.

Prepare for bed as usual. Find a comfy position in bed, and let this meditation lull you to sleep while your body is recovering and re-energizing.

Slowly calm yourself before this healing journey begins. Let's do a short breathing exercise. Breathe through your nose, counting to six. One, two, three, four, five, six. Then exhale through your mouth to the count of ten. One, two, three, four, five, six, seven, eight, nine, ten. If you can't reach those numbers, don't be concerned in any way. Do what is convenient.

Repeat this for a short while. And then, let yourself flow into your natural breathing pattern. While inhaling, imagine you are breathing in a beautiful, glittering light. Breathing out, exhale all worries and negativity. Feel how your body is more and more relaxed with each exhale.

Imagine you are lying in a beautiful, green garden full of colorful flowers. You're listening to insects in grass, birds, and wind in the trees. Feel the peace and serenity.

Now, we'll relax the whole body. Breathe slowly and deeply. Concentrate on your feet. Relax your feet. Relax your toes, heels, whole feet. Relax your ankles, lower legs. Feel your legs relaxing. Relax your knees. Bring your focus to your thighs - the front and the backside of them. Feel how your thighs are more and more relaxed with each exhale. Your toes, heels, and feet - relaxed. Your ankles, lower legs, knees, and thighs - relaxed.

Put your attention to your hips, glutes, and pelvic area. Relax your glutes and observe how, with every breath, your glutes and hips are more relaxed. And, with them, the whole lower half of the body is relaxed, too.

Bring your awareness to your hands. Relax your fingers and palms. Relax your wrists. Relax your forearms, relax your elbows, and your upper arms. Your palms and fingers - relaxed, your wrists - relaxed. Your forearms, elbows, and upper arms - all are relaxed.

Bring your attention to your stomach and chest. Observe how they easily move in the rhythm of your breathing. Relax your chest completely. Relax your stomach. Focus on your lower back. Relax your lower back. Feel the surface under your back, and relax your back, part by part, from the lower back, slowly moving up to the shoulders.

Feel the peace. Feel how your body is giving you thanks for those moments. How much good is happening right now!

Relax your shoulders. The most crucial part of relaxation is the shoulders. Relax them and let them loose. Observe how they are more and more relaxed with every exhale. Notice how, by relaxing the shoulders, you are loosening the whole body. Feel the relief.

Relax your neck. Relax the top of your head. Relax your forehead. Relax your ears. Relax your cheeks. Relax your lips and let your jaw loose. Calm your eyes. Relax eye muscles completely.

Breathe deeply and feel the peace. Your body is relaxed now.

Now, imagine a small, white cloud above you. It's a beautiful cloud, and it's here only for you. It brings you healing. The cloud is right above your head. Are you excited? Do you feel happy about what is coming?

It's beginning to rain from the cloud. It's a rain of light. Feel the drops on your face. It's a healing rain. You can imagine it as you want, like a light, small crystals, or pure water. Connect it with healing.

Your whole head is shining now in healing light. Enjoy it. You know what's going on now. The clod moves down, above your neck. The raindrops fall over your neck. It starts shining, too. Now, your head and the neck shine.

The cloud moves down, above your shoulders, chest, and stomach. Feel the rain. Feel the healing. Watch yourself glowing - your head, neck, shoulders, chest, and stomach. The cloud is expanding above your arms. Your arms and hands begin to shine. The cloud is growing, and now it's above your hips, pelvis, glutes, and genitals. Those parts are shining in the healing light now. Your head is shining, your neck, shoulders, chest, stomach, arms, legs, hips, and glutes. The cloud is moving down, and raindrops are falling over your legs. Observe your legs begin to shine. Do you feel the rain? Can you feel how it serves you and what's its purpose? The white, healing cloud is now above your whole body, and it's the same size as it. It's raining over your whole body, and all the parts are shinning. This moment, the healing raindrops on each part of your body. It's a rain of light, rain of health, and you shine brightly. Say thanks to this moment. Feel grateful for the healing that's happening right now. If you have some health challenges, you can now bring your little white cloud above the par that needs healing. If you don't have any particular health issue, let the rain falls all over your body. Visualize yourself shining.

If you have brought the healing cloud above a particular part of your body, imagine it's lighting. It's shining, and it works perfectly. All the cells of your body are happy to bring back the balance which your body deserves.

Right now, you are giving an incredible gift to your body. The body is thankful, and it is going to show you appreciation. Enjoy this feeling and the insight that healing is going on right now.

Any tension that remains in the body now releases itself in the light's comfort as it spreads through every cell and every atom. As the rain of light drops all over your body, your skin may tingle or feel warm. You feel all the stress and pain draining away under the drops of light.

The soft light is enveloping you and spreading out, warm, and powerful.

Enjoy the relaxation and feeling that the rain brought. Rest in it, allowing it to do its work of healing you. You are filled with pure, loving energy. See the light radiating from the center of your body.

From this relaxed state, while your body is healing itself using infinite wisdom, you can send yourself loving thoughts to support the healing process. It's time to release the old negative thinking patterns that caused disease in your body and to adopt new ones, and build perfect, vibrant health. Listen to my voice as I am repeating positive statements. Allow these ideas to enter your subconscious and help you build positive, new patterns that create health in your body and mind.

Repeat my words mentally or just listen to these affirmations and let them become your new beliefs.

I am healing my body and mind.

I am one with life.

Perfect health is my birthright.

I forgive all those I need to forgive.

I forgive myself.

I feel growing love for myself.

I take care of myself because I love myself.

I am choosing health for my body, mind, and spirit.

I am grateful for my amazing body and all the wonderful things it does every day.

I am grateful for my healthy body and healthy mind.

I am calm and strong.

I am completely healthy.

All the cells of my body are healthy and vibrant.
I am full of positive energy.
I am full of life.
I am loved. I am enough. I am complete.
I am always healing and feel good.
I am letting go of everything that doesn't serve my highest good.
I am letting go of fear. I am letting go of anger, blame, sorrow, guilt, jealousy, blame, tension.
I am in peace. There's no need to struggle.
I am a wonderful expression of life.
I have the power within me, and it's the same power that has created me.
Now, I allow that power to heal my body and mind.
The past has no power over me. I'm letting go of it now.
I am unique and magnificent.
I am worthy of love just because I exist.
I accept and appreciate myself.
I'm willing to heal. I deserve all the best life has to give me. I deserve to be perfectly healthy.
I am in perfect balance and in harmony with the world. I allow divine energy to circulate throughout my body and helps it use higher intelligence to heal.
I am healing my body and mind.
I am one with life.
Perfect health is my birthright.
I forgive all those I need to forgive.
I forgive myself.
I feel growing love for myself.
I take care of myself because I love myself.
I am choosing health for my body, mind, and spirit.
I am grateful for my amazing body and all the wonderful things it does every day.
I am grateful for my healthy body and healthy mind.
I am calm and strong.
I am completely healthy.
All the cells of my body are healthy and vibrant.
I am full of positive energy.
I am full of life.
I am loved. I am enough. I am complete.
I am always healing and feel good.
I am letting go of everything that doesn't serve my highest good.
I am letting go of fear. I am letting go of anger, blame, sorrow, guilt, jealousy, blame, tension.
I am in peace. There's no need to struggle.
I am a wonderful expression of life.
I have the power within me, and it's the same power that has created me.
Now, I allow that power to heal my body and mind.
The past has no power over me. I'm letting go of it now.
I am unique and magnificent.
I am worthy of love just because I exist.
I accept and appreciate myself.
I'm willing to heal. I deserve all the best life has to give me. I deserve to be perfectly healthy.
I am in perfect balance and in harmony with the world. I allow divine energy to circulate throughout my body and helps it use higher intelligence to heal.

Take a nice, deep breath and exhale, visualizing flowers and grass around you.
Sleep well, and have sweet dreams, while your body is healing and reenergizing. Good night!

# Affirmations for reprogramming your subconsciousness while sleeping

150 min

Welcome to the affirmations while sleeping.
You can listen to them when you are about to sleep.
Also, listen to these affirmations when you fall asleep.
They are incredibly powerful. Thanks to affirmations, we have created our beliefs.
Unfortunately, most of our beliefs don't serve us anymore.
Listening to these affirmations, you have an opportunity to reprogram your subconsciousness and create new beliefs that will serve your highest good, so you could create a new reality you love.
Enjoy your new beliefs, relax, and fall asleep.
Breathe deeply and slowly, relaxed and ready for a wonderful, refreshing sleep.
You can repeat affirmations mentally, but you don't have to.
Let's begin.
I feel grateful for all the possibilities.
I'm proud of my achievements.
I feel peace and serenity.
I believe in myself.
My mind is calm now.
My heart is grateful.
My heart is pure.
My body is relaxed now.
I feel safe and confident.
It's a new day tomorrow, full of new possibilities.
I know I deserve this rest and relaxation.
Everything's good in my world.
In my world, everything happens for my highest good.
Life loves and supports me.
I'm perfectly healthy, and all the cells in my body are renewed each day.
Everything I do, I do with love, ease, and joy.
I feel great.
I'm full of energy.
My mind is relaxed.
My body feels the peace.
I have a positive mindset.
All of my cells are full of love and light.
I let go of the past and look at the future.
I enjoy my life.
Life is wonderful.
My heart is open, and I radiate love.
I look at everything with love, and I love what I see.
When I give love, I get love in return.
Wherever I go, I find love.
I know I deserve the very best.

Everything I touch turns into success.
I am a money magnet.
I attract abundance.
My income raises all the time.
I love this abundance. I have enough money for everything I need and want.
I do the work I love, and it brings me abundance.
I successfully manage all my tasks, so I do everything with joy.
In my world, everything's good.
I give my light to this world.
I know I'm worthy.
I enjoy being myself.
I live in the present.
I inhale peace. I exhale tension.
Wonderful things are waiting for me.
I let go of any anger.
I forgive myself for all the mistakes.
I forgive everyone who needs my forgiveness.
I refuse to give up.
All the issues are getting away from my path.
I know I'm divinely protected and guided.
I accept diversity and other people's opinions.
I know there is a good reason why I'm here.
I surround myself with great people.
Everything I do, I do with love.
I have self-confidence.
I know what I deserve.
Deep in myself, I feel peace, serenity, and blessings.
Everything's simple.
I know I'm a winner.
I accept myself completely.
I always see the best in others.
Things are always happening for my highest good.
I feel happy.
I'm the creator of my reality.
I see abundance everywhere.
I am a money magnet.
I deserve to be wealthy.
Money easily comes into my life.
I know I'm guided.
Today I witness miracles.
I live my dream life.
I achieve everything I want.
I love life.
I believe in myself.
My dreams are bigger than my fears.
I can't be unsuccessful.
I deserve to make my dreams come true.
Something unbelievable is about to happen.
Everything always works for me.

I choose happiness.
I let go of worries and fears.
I am love.
I love life, and life loves me in return.
I am able to create my perfect reality.
My heart is thankful.
I enjoy my relationships, which are full of love, support, and respect.
I radiate happiness.
My life is full of joy.
I live an incredible love story.
Love is the basis of all of my relationships.
Everything's good.
I refuse to give up.
I know my inner wisdom is guiding me in my choices.
I love my family.
I show my loved ones how much I care.
My life is full of abundance.
I feel thankfulness for all the options today.
I'm proud of my achievements.
I feel peace and serenity.
I trust myself.
My mind is calm.
My heart is grateful.
My heart is pure.
My body is relaxed now.
I feel safe and confident.
It's a new day tomorrow, full of new possibilities.
I know I deserve this rest and relaxation.
Everything's good in my world.
In my world, everything happens for my highest good.
Life loves and supports me.
I'm perfectly healthy, and all the cells in my body are renewed each day.
Everything I do, I do with love, ease, and joy.
I feel great.
I'm full of energy.
My mind is relaxed.
My body feels the peace.
I have a positive mindset.
All of my cells are full of love and light.
I let go of the past and look at the future.
I enjoy my life.
Life is wonderful.
My heart is open, and I radiate love.
I look at everything with love, and I love what I see.
When I give love, I get love in return.
Wherever I go, I find love.
I know I deserve the very best.
Everything I touch turns into success.
I am a money magnet.

I attract abundance.
My income raises all the time.
I love this abundance. I have enough money for everything I need and want.
I do the work I love, and it brings me abundance.
I successfully manage all my tasks, so I do everything with joy.
In my world, everything's good.
I give my light to this world.
I know I'm worthy.
I enjoy being myself.
I live in the present.
I inhale peace. I exhale tension.
Wonderful things are waiting for me.
I let go of any anger.
I forgive myself for all the mistakes.
I forgive everyone who needs my forgiveness.
I refuse to give up.
All the issues are getting away from my path.
I know I'm divinely protected and guided.
I accept diversity and other people's opinions.
I know there is a good reason why I'm here.
I surround myself with great people.
Everything I do, I do with love.
I have self-confidence.
I know what I deserve.
Deep in myself, I feel peace, serenity, and blessings.
Everything's simple.
I know I'm a winner.
I accept myself completely.
I always see the best in others.
Things are always happening for my highest good.
I feel happy.
I'm the creator of my reality.
I see abundance everywhere.
I am a money magnet.
I deserve to be wealthy.
Money easily comes into my life.
I know I'm guided.
Today I witness miracles.
I live my dream life.
I achieve everything I want.
I love life.
I believe in myself.
My dreams are bigger than my fears.
I can't be unsuccessful.
I deserve to make my dreams come true.
Something unbelievable is about to happen.
Everything always works for me.
I choose happiness.
I let go of worries and fears.

I am love.
I love life, and life loves me in return.
I am able to create my perfect reality.
My heart is thankful.
I enjoy my relationships, which are full of love, support, and respect.
I feel grateful for all the possibilities.
I'm proud of my achievements.
I feel peace and serenity.
I believe in myself.
My mind is calm now.
My heart is grateful.
My heart is pure.
My body is relaxed now.
I feel safe and confident.
It's a new day tomorrow, full of new possibilities.
I know I deserve this rest and relaxation.
Everything's good in my world.
In my world, everything happens for my highest good.
Life loves and supports me.
I'm perfectly healthy, and all the cells in my body are renewed each day.
Everything I do, I do with love, ease, and joy.
I feel great.
I'm full of energy.
My mind is relaxed.
My body feels the peace.
I have a positive mindset.
All of my cells are full of love and light.
I let go of the past and look at the future.
I enjoy my life.
Life is wonderful.
My heart is open, and I radiate love.
I look at everything with love, and I love what I see.
When I give love, I get love in return.
Wherever I go, I find love.
I know I deserve the very best.
Everything I touch turns into success.
I am a money magnet.
I attract abundance.
My income raises all the time.
I love this abundance. I have enough money for everything I need and want.
I do the work I love, and it brings me abundance.
I successfully manage all my tasks, so I do everything with joy.
In my world, everything's good.
I give my light to this world.
I know I'm worthy.
I enjoy being myself.
I live in the present.
I inhale peace. I exhale tension.
Wonderful things are waiting for me.

I let go of any anger.
I forgive myself for all the mistakes.
I forgive everyone who needs my forgiveness.
I refuse to give up.
All the issues are getting away from my path.
I know I'm divinely protected and guided.
I accept diversity and other people's opinions.
I know there is a good reason why I'm here.
I surround myself with great people.
Everything I do, I do with love.
I have self-confidence.
I know what I deserve.
Deep in myself, I feel peace, serenity, and blessings.
Everything's simple.
I know I'm a winner.
I accept myself completely.
I always see the best in others.
Things are always happening for my highest good.
I feel happy.
I'm the creator of my reality.
I see abundance everywhere.
I am a money magnet.
I deserve to be wealthy.
Money easily comes into my life.
I know I'm guided.
Today I witness miracles.
I live my dream life.
I achieve everything I want.
I love life.
I believe in myself.
My dreams are bigger than my fears.
I can't be unsuccessful.
I deserve to make my dreams come true.
Something unbelievable is about to happen.
Everything always works for me.
I choose happiness.
I let go of worries and fears.
I am love.
I love life, and life loves me in return.
I am able to create my perfect reality.
My heart is thankful.
I enjoy my relationships, which are full of love, support, and respect.
I radiate happiness.
My life is full of joy.
I live an incredible love story.
Love is the basis of all of my relationships.
Everything's good.
I refuse to give up.
I know my inner wisdom is guiding me in my choices.

I love my family.
I show my loved ones how much I care.
My life is full of abundance.
I feel grateful for all the possibilities.
I'm proud of my achievements.
I feel peace and serenity.
I believe in myself.
My mind is calm now.
My heart is grateful.
My heart is pure.
My body is relaxed now.
I feel safe and confident.
It's a new day tomorrow, full of new possibilities.
I know I deserve this rest and relaxation.
Everything's good in my world.
In my world, everything happens for my highest good.
Life loves and supports me.
I'm perfectly healthy, and all the cells in my body are renewed each day.
Everything I do, I do with love, ease, and joy.
I feel great.
I'm full of energy.
My mind is relaxed.
My body feels the peace.
I have a positive mindset.
All of my cells are full of love and light.
I let go of the past and look at the future.
I enjoy my life.
Life is wonderful.
My heart is open, and I radiate love.
I look at everything with love, and I love what I see.
When I give love, I get love in return.
Wherever I go, I find love.
I know I deserve the very best.
Everything I touch turns into success.
I am a money magnet.
I attract abundance.
My income raises all the time.
I love this abundance. I have enough money for everything I need and want.
I do the work I love, and it brings me abundance.
I successfully manage all my tasks, so I do everything with joy.
In my world, everything's good.
I give my light to this world.
I know I'm worthy.
I enjoy being myself.
I live in the present.
I inhale peace. I exhale tension.
Wonderful things are waiting for me.
I let go of any anger.
I forgive myself for all the mistakes.

I forgive everyone who needs my forgiveness.
I refuse to give up.
All the issues are getting away from my path.
I know I'm divinely protected and guided.
I accept diversity and other people's opinions.
I know there is a good reason why I'm here.
I surround myself with great people.
Everything I do, I do with love.
I have self-confidence.
I know what I deserve.
Deep in myself, I feel peace, serenity, and blessings.
Everything's simple.
I know I'm a winner.
I accept myself completely.
I always see the best in others.
Things are always happening for my highest good.
I feel happy.
I'm the creator of my reality.
I see abundance everywhere.
I am a money magnet.
I deserve to be wealthy.
Money easily comes into my life.
I know I'm guided.
Today I witness miracles.
I live my dream life.
I achieve everything I want.
I love life.
I believe in myself.
My dreams are bigger than my fears.
I can't be unsuccessful.
I deserve to make my dreams come true.
Something unbelievable is about to happen.
Everything always works for me.
I choose happiness.
I let go of worries and fears.
I am love.
I love life, and life loves me in return.
I am able to create my perfect reality.
My heart is thankful.
I enjoy my relationships, which are full of love, support, and respect.
I radiate happiness.
My life is full of joy.
I live an incredible love story.
Love is the basis of all of my relationships.
Everything's good.
I refuse to give up.
I know my inner wisdom is guiding me in my choices.
I love my family.
I show my loved ones how much I care.

My life is full of abundance.
I feel grateful for all the possibilities.
I'm proud of my achievements.
I feel peace and serenity.
I believe in myself.
My mind is calm now.
My heart is grateful.
My heart is pure.
My body is relaxed now.
I feel safe and confident.
It's a new day tomorrow, full of new possibilities.
I know I deserve this rest and relaxation.
Everything's good in my world.
In my world, everything happens for my highest good.
Life loves and supports me.
I'm perfectly healthy, and all the cells in my body are renewed each day.
Everything I do, I do with love, ease, and joy.
I feel great.
I'm full of energy.
My mind is relaxed.
My body feels the peace.
I have a positive mindset.
All of my cells are full of love and light.
I let go of the past and look at the future.
I enjoy my life.
Life is wonderful.
My heart is open, and I radiate love.
I look at everything with love, and I love what I see.
When I give love, I get love in return.
Wherever I go, I find love.
I know I deserve the very best.
Everything I touch turns into success.
I am a money magnet.
I attract abundance.
My income raises all the time.
I love this abundance. I have enough money for everything I need and want.
I do the work I love, and it brings me abundance.
I successfully manage all my tasks, so I do everything with joy.
In my world, everything's good.
I give my light to this world.
I know I'm worthy.
I enjoy being myself.
I live in the present.
I inhale peace. I exhale tension.
Wonderful things are waiting for me.
I let go of any anger.
I forgive myself for all the mistakes.
I forgive everyone who needs my forgiveness.
I refuse to give up.

All the issues are getting away from my path.
I know I'm divinely protected and guided.
I accept diversity and other people's opinions.
I know there is a good reason why I'm here.
I surround myself with great people.
Everything I do, I do with love.
I have self-confidence.
I know what I deserve.
Deep in myself, I feel peace, serenity, and blessings.
Everything's simple.
I know I'm a winner.
I accept myself completely.
I always see the best in others.
Things are always happening for my highest good.
I feel happy.
I'm the creator of my reality.
I see abundance everywhere.
I am a money magnet.
I deserve to be wealthy.
Money easily comes into my life.
I know I'm guided.
Today I witness miracles.
I live my dream life.
I achieve everything I want.
I love life.
I believe in myself.
My dreams are bigger than my fears.
I can't be unsuccessful.
I deserve to make my dreams come true.
Something unbelievable is about to happen.
Everything always works for me.
I choose happiness.
I let go of worries and fears.
I am love.
I love life, and life loves me in return.
I am able to create my perfect reality.
My heart is thankful.
I enjoy my relationships, which are full of love, support, and respect.
I radiate happiness.
My life is full of joy.
I live an incredible love story.
Love is the basis of all of my relationships.
Everything's good.
I refuse to give up.
I know my inner wisdom is guiding me in my choices.
I love my family.
I show my loved ones how much I care.
My life is full of abundance.
I feel thankfulness for all the options today.

I'm proud of my achievements.
I feel peace and serenity.
I trust myself.
My mind is calm.
My heart is grateful.
My heart is pure.
My body is relaxed now.
I feel safe and confident.
It's a new day tomorrow, full of new possibilities.
I know I deserve this rest and relaxation.
Everything's good in my world.
In my world, everything happens for my highest good.
Life loves and supports me.
I'm perfectly healthy, and all the cells in my body are renewed each day.
Everything I do, I do with love, ease, and joy.
I feel great.
I'm full of energy.
My mind is relaxed.
My body feels the peace.
I have a positive mindset.
All of my cells are full of love and light.
I let go of the past and look at the future.
I enjoy my life.
Life is wonderful.
My heart is open, and I radiate love.
I look at everything with love, and I love what I see.
When I give love, I get love in return.
Wherever I go, I find love.
I know I deserve the very best.
Everything I touch turns into success.
I am a money magnet.
I attract abundance.
My income raises all the time.
I love this abundance. I have enough money for everything I need and want.
I do the work I love, and it brings me abundance.
I successfully manage all my tasks, so I do everything with joy.
In my world, everything's good.
I give my light to this world.
I know I'm worthy.
I enjoy being myself.
I live in the present.
I inhale peace. I exhale tension.
Wonderful things are waiting for me.
I let go of any anger.
I forgive myself for all the mistakes.
I forgive everyone who needs my forgiveness.
I refuse to give up.
All the issues are getting away from my path.
I know I'm divinely protected and guided.

I accept diversity and other people's opinions.
I know there is a good reason why I'm here.
I surround myself with great people.
Everything I do, I do with love.
I have self-confidence.
I know what I deserve.
Deep in myself, I feel peace, serenity, and blessings.
Everything's simple.
I know I'm a winner.
I accept myself completely.
I always see the best in others.
Things are always happening for my highest good.
I feel happy.
I'm the creator of my reality.
I see abundance everywhere.
I am a money magnet.
I deserve to be wealthy.
Money easily comes into my life.
I know I'm guided.
Today I witness miracles.
I live my dream life.
I achieve everything I want.
I love life.
I believe in myself.
My dreams are bigger than my fears.
I can't be unsuccessful.
I deserve to make my dreams come true.
Something unbelievable is about to happen.
Everything always works for me.
I choose happiness.
I let go of worries and fears.
I am love.
I love life, and life loves me in return.
I am able to create my perfect reality.
My heart is thankful.
I enjoy my relationships, which are full of love, support, and respect.
I feel grateful for all the possibilities.
I'm proud of my achievements.
I feel peace and serenity.
I believe in myself.
My mind is calm now.
My heart is grateful.
My heart is pure.
My body is relaxed now.
I feel safe and confident.
It's a new day tomorrow, full of new possibilities.
I know I deserve this rest and relaxation.
Everything's good in my world.
In my world, everything happens for my highest good.

Life loves and supports me.
I'm perfectly healthy, and all the cells in my body are renewed each day.
Everything I do, I do with love, ease, and joy.
I feel great.
I'm full of energy.
My mind is relaxed.
My body feels the peace.
I have a positive mindset.
All of my cells are full of love and light.
I let go of the past and look at the future.
I enjoy my life.
Life is wonderful.
My heart is open, and I radiate love.
I look at everything with love, and I love what I see.
When I give love, I get love in return.
Wherever I go, I find love.
I know I deserve the very best.
Everything I touch turns into success.
I am a money magnet.
I attract abundance.
My income raises all the time.
I love this abundance. I have enough money for everything I need and want.
I do the work I love, and it brings me abundance.
I successfully manage all my tasks, so I do everything with joy.
In my world, everything's good.
I give my light to this world.
I know I'm worthy.
I enjoy being myself.
I live in the present.
I inhale peace. I exhale tension.
Wonderful things are waiting for me.
I let go of any anger.
I forgive myself for all the mistakes.
I forgive everyone who needs my forgiveness.
I refuse to give up.
All the issues are getting away from my path.
I know I'm divinely protected and guided.
I accept diversity and other people's opinions.
I know there is a good reason why I'm here.
I surround myself with great people.
Everything I do, I do with love.
I have self-confidence.
I know what I deserve.
Deep in myself, I feel peace, serenity, and blessings.
Everything's simple.
I know I'm a winner.
I accept myself completely.
I always see the best in others.
Things are always happening for my highest good.

I accept diversity and other people's opinions.
I know there is a good reason why I'm here.
I surround myself with great people.
Everything I do, I do with love.
I have self-confidence.
I know what I deserve.
Deep in myself, I feel peace, serenity, and blessings.
Everything's simple.
I know I'm a winner.
I accept myself completely.
I always see the best in others.
Things are always happening for my highest good.
I feel happy.
I'm the creator of my reality.
I see abundance everywhere.
I am a money magnet.
I deserve to be wealthy.
Money easily comes into my life.
I know I'm guided.
Today I witness miracles.
I live my dream life.
I achieve everything I want.
I love life.
I believe in myself.
My dreams are bigger than my fears.
I can't be unsuccessful.
I deserve to make my dreams come true.
Something unbelievable is about to happen.
Everything always works for me.
I choose happiness.
I let go of worries and fears.
I am love.
I love life, and life loves me in return.
I am able to create my perfect reality.
My heart is thankful.
I enjoy my relationships, which are full of love, support, and respect.
I feel grateful for all the possibilities.
I'm proud of my achievements.
I feel peace and serenity.
I believe in myself.
My mind is calm now.
My heart is grateful.
My heart is pure.
My body is relaxed now.
I feel safe and confident.
It's a new day tomorrow, full of new possibilities.
I know I deserve this rest and relaxation.
Everything's good in my world.
In my world, everything happens for my highest good.

Life loves and supports me.
I'm perfectly healthy, and all the cells in my body are renewed each day.
Everything I do, I do with love, ease, and joy.
I feel great.
I'm full of energy.
My mind is relaxed.
My body feels the peace.
I have a positive mindset.
All of my cells are full of love and light.
I let go of the past and look at the future.
I enjoy my life.
Life is wonderful.
My heart is open, and I radiate love.
I look at everything with love, and I love what I see.
When I give love, I get love in return.
Wherever I go, I find love.
I know I deserve the very best.
Everything I touch turns into success.
I am a money magnet.
I attract abundance.
My income raises all the time.
I love this abundance. I have enough money for everything I need and want.
I do the work I love, and it brings me abundance.
I successfully manage all my tasks, so I do everything with joy.
In my world, everything's good.
I give my light to this world.
I know I'm worthy.
I enjoy being myself.
I live in the present.
I inhale peace. I exhale tension.
Wonderful things are waiting for me.
I let go of any anger.
I forgive myself for all the mistakes.
I forgive everyone who needs my forgiveness.
I refuse to give up.
All the issues are getting away from my path.
I know I'm divinely protected and guided.
I accept diversity and other people's opinions.
I know there is a good reason why I'm here.
I surround myself with great people.
Everything I do, I do with love.
I have self-confidence.
I know what I deserve.
Deep in myself, I feel peace, serenity, and blessings.
Everything's simple.
I know I'm a winner.
I accept myself completely.
I always see the best in others.
Things are always happening for my highest good.

I feel happy.
I'm the creator of my reality.
I see abundance everywhere.
I am a money magnet.
I deserve to be wealthy.
Money easily comes into my life.
I know I'm guided.
Today I witness miracles.
I live my dream life.
I achieve everything I want.
I love life.
I believe in myself.
My dreams are bigger than my fears.
I can't be unsuccessful.
I deserve to make my dreams come true.
Something unbelievable is about to happen.
Everything always works for me.
I choose happiness.
I let go of worries and fears.
I am love.
I love life, and life loves me in return.
I am able to create my perfect reality.
My heart is thankful.
I enjoy my relationships, which are full of love, support, and respect.
I radiate happiness.
My life is full of joy.
I live an incredible love story.
Love is the basis of all of my relationships.
Everything's good.
I refuse to give up.
I know my inner wisdom is guiding me in my choices.
I love my family.
I show my loved ones how much I care.
My life is full of abundance.
I feel grateful for all the possibilities.
I'm proud of my achievements.
I feel peace and serenity.
I believe in myself.
My mind is calm now.
My heart is grateful.
My heart is pure.
My body is relaxed now.
I feel safe and confident.
It's a new day tomorrow, full of new possibilities.
I know I deserve this rest and relaxation.
Everything's good in my world.
In my world, everything happens for my highest good.
Life loves and supports me.
I'm perfectly healthy, and all the cells in my body are renewed each day.

Everything I do, I do with love, ease, and joy.
I feel great.
I'm full of energy.
My mind is relaxed.
My body feels the peace.
I have a positive mindset.
All of my cells are full of love and light.
I let go of the past and look at the future.
I enjoy my life.
Life is wonderful.
My heart is open, and I radiate love.
I look at everything with love, and I love what I see.
When I give love, I get love in return.
Wherever I go, I find love.
I know I deserve the very best.
Everything I touch turns into success.
I am a money magnet.
I attract abundance.
My income raises all the time.
I love this abundance. I have enough money for everything I need and want.
I do the work I love, and it brings me abundance.
I successfully manage all my tasks, so I do everything with joy.
In my world, everything's good.
I give my light to this world.
I know I'm worthy.
I enjoy being myself.
I live in the present.
I inhale peace. I exhale tension.
Wonderful things are waiting for me.
I let go of any anger.
I forgive myself for all the mistakes.
I forgive everyone who needs my forgiveness.
I refuse to give up.
All the issues are getting away from my path.
I know I'm divinely protected and guided.
I accept diversity and other people's opinions.
I know there is a good reason why I'm here.
I surround myself with great people.
Everything I do, I do with love.
I have self-confidence.
I know what I deserve.
Deep in myself, I feel peace, serenity, and blessings.
Everything's simple.
I know I'm a winner.
I accept myself completely.
I always see the best in others.
Things are always happening for my highest good.
I feel happy.
I'm the creator of my reality.

I see abundance everywhere.
I am a money magnet.
I deserve to be wealthy.
Money easily comes into my life.
I know I'm guided.
Today I witness miracles.
I live my dream life.
I achieve everything I want.
I love life.
I believe in myself.
My dreams are bigger than my fears.
I can't be unsuccessful.
I deserve to make my dreams come true.
Something unbelievable is about to happen.
Everything always works for me.
I choose happiness.
I let go of worries and fears.
I am love.
I love life, and life loves me in return.
I am able to create my perfect reality.
My heart is thankful.
I enjoy my relationships, which are full of love, support, and respect.
I radiate happiness.
My life is full of joy.
I live an incredible love story.
Love is the basis of all of my relationships.
Everything's good.
I refuse to give up.
I know my inner wisdom is guiding me in my choices.
I love my family.
I show my loved ones how much I care.
My life is full of abundance.

www.ingramcontent.com/pod-product-compliance
Lightning Source LLC
Chambersburg PA
CBHW081507080526
44589CB00017B/2684

I see abundance everywhere.
I am a money magnet.
I deserve to be wealthy.
Money easily comes into my life.
I know I'm guided.
Today I witness miracles.
I live my dream life.
I achieve everything I want.
I love life.
I believe in myself.
My dreams are bigger than my fears.
I can't be unsuccessful.
I deserve to make my dreams come true.
Something unbelievable is about to happen.
Everything always works for me.
I choose happiness.
I let go of worries and fears.
I am love.
I love life, and life loves me in return.
I am able to create my perfect reality.
My heart is thankful.
I enjoy my relationships, which are full of love, support, and respect.
I radiate happiness.
My life is full of joy.
I live an incredible love story.
Love is the basis of all of my relationships.
Everything's good.
I refuse to give up.
I know my inner wisdom is guiding me in my choices.
I love my family.
I show my loved ones how much I care.
My life is full of abundance.

www.ingramcontent.com/pod-product-compliance
Lightning Source LLC
Chambersburg PA
CBHW081507080526
44589CB00017B/2684